MW01701533

Written by Wendy Ellen Hanophy
Photos and Illustrations by Brian Sauriol

Published 2026 by Satiama Publishing, a service mark of Satiama LLC
PO Box 1636
Palmer Lake, CO 80133
satiamapublishing.com
customerservice@satiamapublishing.com

For more information or for permissions, please contact us at customerservice@satiamapublishing.com

Printed in the United States of America

ISBN E-book Edition: 979-8-9994573-9-4

ISBN Paperback Edition: 979-8-9994573-8-7

Library of Congress Control Number: 2026939726

BISAC Subject Codes

OCC037000: MIND, BODY, SPIRIT / Feng Shui OCC033000:

MIND, BODY, SPIRIT / Gaia & Earth Energies OCC014000:

MIND, BODY, SPIRIT / New Thought

Printed in the United States of America

WIND, WATER, AND WING

FENG SHUI AND THE NATURE OF HOME

WENDY ELLEN HANOPHY

Satiama
PUBLISHING

TABLE OF CONTENTS

PART TWO
THE SACRED GEOGRAPHY OF PLACE

PART THREE
THE HOUSE THAT BREATHES

PART FOUR
KINSHIP BEYOND THE DOOR

PART FIVE
RESTORING FLOW

WHAT READERS ARE SAYING

"*Wind, Water, and Wing* is a radiant source of wisdom and inspiration. Open it to any page and be transported into the heart of Nature's healing presence. Wendy Hanophy's essential observations and lyrical voice reveal how intimately connected we are to our natural world and built environments. Her book offers us wise counsel and experiential practices to step fully into a sacred relationship with Nature and our place in it."

Terah Kathryn Collins, best-selling author of *The Western Guide to Feng Shui*

"In *Wind, Water, and Wing,* Wendy Hanophy offers a deeply grounded and timely vision for living in right relationship with the natural world. She carefully describes how the fundamental forces of nature shape not only our landscapes and homes but also our communities and inner lives. Her resonant words encourage us to observe more closely, listen more deeply, and align our daily choices with the living systems that sustain us.

Hanophy's transformative engagement with the forces that support life is charming, and I found myself returning to poetic passages about a tiny, precisely placed hummingbird nest, or the timeless conversations of wind and water.

I strongly recommend this book to all who long for a deeper connection to Earth, and who want concrete, inspiring ways to make that connection real. *Wind, Water, and Wing* is a companion, a catalyst, and a call to stewardship that we urgently need."

David Wann, bestselling author of *Affluenza* and *Simple Prosperity*

"I love this book! It is the book I always hoped someone would write, a way to 'be' with the structures we live in, the earth we live in and on, and the relationship between them all. It is lyrically written, but has a practicality that is understandable. Each time I sat down to read a part of the book, I instantly relaxed and walked away with a quiet mind, which is something we all need. I love that it isn't preachy or written as something that will instantly change your life, but rather a way of understanding and being with intention and honor."

— *Dianne Pavelka*

"Beautifully written, meditative, and hopeful, this book brings connection to ourselves and our relationship with the Earth in a way that is gentle, accessible, and urgently needed."

— *Crystal Andrews*

"Reading the final page of *Wind, Water and Wing* last night, I realized that Wendy's gift of transforming science and the natural world into memorable prose, mini vignettes of outward listening (versus inward meditation) and her reasoned optimism, caused a profound shift in my own awareness, changing my personal understanding of relationship with our world.

For me, *Wind, Water, and Wing* is a lyrical toolbox that helps solidify those "feelings" into actionable awareness. Awareness that has the potential to inspire proper stewardship of our world, enhancing the relationship between all life, one human at a time."

—*Debbie Alther*

BEFORE YOU BEGIN

You may wish to keep a blank journal nearby as you journey through these pages. The Reflections and Practices offered here are not meant to be hurried through or completed in a single sitting. Instead, they are invitations meant to be returned to, contemplated across the changing seasons of life, and lived with slowly.

Move gently. Pause when a passage stirs something within you. Write down your thoughts, your questions, and the small promises you make to yourself along the way.

This book is not a river rushing toward its final page, but a quiet stream winding through the landscape. It invites you to experience Feng Shui as a living, reciprocal relationship with the world around you. Wander its banks. Linger at each bend. Allow every idea, reflection, and practice to unfold in its own rhythm.

Trust the timing of what reveals itself.

PROLOGUE: WHY WIND AND WATER STILL MATTER

No one sets out to be a heretic.

I did not question science when I first entered the study of wildlife biology; I trusted it. I accepted the methods, the models, the rules meant to keep inquiry clean and objective. We were taught to be careful with language, to avoid anthropomorphism, to strip our observations of feeling and intention. The goal was clarity.

But somewhere in that effort, something vital was thinned.

Living beings became study subjects. Relationships became mechanisms. Intelligence was quietly narrowed to what could be measured, as if thought, feeling, memory, and meaning belonged only to humans. In trying to avoid projection, we flattened the living world into objects—useful, fascinating, but somehow less alive than we were.

At the same time, my early encounters with Feng Shui were often clothed in a different kind of certainty: rules, prescriptions, promised outcomes. Place this here. Remove that from there. Harmony as a result to be achieved rather than a relationship to be tended. While these techniques held genuine wisdom, I felt an unease I couldn't yet name. Something essential was missing.

What both traditions had lost, at their worst, was humility.

What both revealed, at their best, was listening.

Science, when practiced deeply, does not deny relationships; it reveals them. Air is not inert chemistry but a moving medium shaped by forests and oceans, by lungs and leaves. Water is not a resource but a memory-bearing flow, binding cloud to river, body to soil. Life is not isolated; it is responsive.

Feng Shui, in its original form, spoke the same truth. It was never about control or fortune. It was about orientation. Learning how wind moves, how water gathers, how life settles into patterns that support or strain the whole. It was a way of helping people remember themselves as participants in a living field.

Many of us no longer feel that participation.

We work in buildings sealed from the weather. We move through landscapes at speed. We live surrounded by objects, screens, and systems designed for efficiency, yet we carry a quiet sense of disconnection we cannot name. We long to feel grounded, but rarely touch the ground. We seek balance, but measure it in outcomes rather than attention.

This book grows from that recognition.

It is about ecology, yes, but not ecology as abstraction or crisis alone. And it is about Feng Shui, but not as a system of fixes or fortunes. It is about relationship: how humans, homes, and landscapes participate in the same living patterns, whether we are paying attention or not.

I am not interested in offering readers solutions that come from outside themselves, nor in positioning Feng Shui as a way to "fix" people, homes, or lives. How can we hope to heal our relationship with the Earth if we have not learned to listen to our own bodies? How can we restore balance in the world if we refuse to practice it within ourselves?

Healing, I have come to understand, is not imposed. It emerges through restored flow, through attention, responsiveness, and care.

Qi is not a metaphor here. It is movement itself: the pulse that threads through muscle and breath, through rooms and watersheds, through migrating birds and the beams that hold a roof. When that movement stagnates, whether in a body, a home, or a landscape, life suffers. When it flows, life adapts.

This book asks a different set of questions.

Not *How can I make this place work for me?*

But *How can I move in a way that allows this place to thrive?*

That question has shaped every page that follows. It shifts authority away from domination and toward reciprocity. It reminds us that responsibility need not arrive as guilt or shame, but as recognition. It's the moment we realize our choices ripple outward, into soil and water and air, and inward, into our own breath.

The birds have been my teachers in this. Their attention is precise. Their presence is responsive. They do not impose themselves on the world; they reply to it. They remind us that perception itself is an ecological act.

Every breath is part of a conversation older than words. Every act of care is a way of saying *I remember.*

The wind still moves through us. The water still carries its message. We are still part of the pattern if we choose to listen.

When the Wind and Water Spoke...

Long before anyone hung a wind chime or placed a mirror to deflect bad energy, there was the wind, threading through reeds, across the skin of rivers, and through the fur, feather, and leaf it brushed in passing. The world breathed with the wind, every creature rising and settling on its quiet rhythm.

The wind carried a message, and the waters remembered it, echoing its secrets in ripples, currents, and tides.

Water spoke the message to the land, rounding stones, deepening canyons, pooling in the small depressions for new life to begin. Water did not seek perfection, no fixed shape or flawless path. It sought connection and belonging, filling every hollow, threading into every root, binding the living world together.

Feng Shui began there, in the living grammar of the Earth. Wind and water shaping stone, shaping forest, shaping us. The ancients listened to the conversation of wind and water, knowing their lives were sustained by the same breath that sways trees and turns the curve of dunes, and shaped by the same waters that carried seeds and food. They sought to dwell in reciprocity with the land. A home was sited where wind and water danced kindly together. A village prospered because the people paid attention to slope and sun, to birds' flight, to how the mist rose from the valley floor. To practice Feng Shui was to live knowing that everything holds a direction, a rhythm, a pulse, and that our own bodies echo that same pattern.

We used to know this. The birds still do.

They are the quiet masters of Feng Shui. Watch them for long enough, and you see how they build not in the prettiest place, but in the right one. They know where the morning sun warms the eggs, where wind won't scatter the nest, and where water lies near enough for life. They live by attunement, not intention.

The birds have always been our first geomancers, reading the invisible, their flight patterns tracing the contours of unseen currents. They know where and when to land, when to rise, how to ride the currents with the wind's persuasion.

What if Feng Shui was never meant to be a human invention at all, but an observation that the world arranges itself beautifully when left to its own intelligence? That balance is already present in how a stream finds its course, or how light bends around a leaf.

This book is for remembering that intelligence, not just through walls and rooms, but through the shared insight of the more-than-human world. Feng shui was easily mastered by the birds, who shape their lives by wind, water, and the curve of the earth. They practice it still, in every lift of wing and turn of feather. If we can feel the subtle currents as they do, we, too, may find our place within the greater flow.

FENG SHUI: A WORKING DEFINITION

> *Feng Shui is the art of belonging. At its essence, feng shui is the study of how our environments shape the quality of our lives, and how, in turn, our lives are mirrored in the spaces we create. Rather than prescribing how a space should be arranged, it invites awareness, intention, and relationship.*

PART ONE
REMEMBERING THE LANGUAGE OF WIND AND WATER

Before language began to constrict what we could feel or say, and before our attention turned outward to seek guidance rather than inward for knowing, we lived in intimate contact with the world. Wind on our skin, the shift of a bird's call, the scent of rain approaching, all spoke to us with clarity. This section invites a return to that older literacy, the one carried in breath and bone. Here we remember how to listen, how to feel our way back into relationship again, and how to recognize ourselves as part of the living Earth that has held us from the beginning.

CHAPTER ONE

WHEN WE STOPPED NOTICING

Somewhere along the way, our intentions grew bolder than our attention, and we began to believe we could shape the world without listening to it.

Somewhere between the hum of highways and the glow of screens, we forgot how to feel the air moving through us. We traded the pulse of seasons for the clock's insistence, the scent of rain through an open window for the hum of ventilation. The world did not stop speaking. Our awareness simply grew thin.

We spoke over the wind and screamed over the water, mistaking our schemes for belonging. Walls rose, rivers were straightened, trees felled to make room for our need to see farther than our eyes were meant to see. We shut the wind out, then wondered why the air inside grew stale.

And yet, the wind still finds its way in, through cracks and open windows, through the songs of sparrows nesting under eaves. Even in our noise and haste, the old teachers persist. The wind brushes against our faces, trying to remind us of its shape. The water traces its patient script beneath the pavement, whispering the same lesson it has offered since the beginning. Flow around, not through.

Feng Shui can be renewed in these small acts of remembering: in opening a window, in turning our faces toward the wind, in letting the senses relearn the world. This chapter is not about technique, but about recovering the capacity to notice. It begins with a single humble question. What does this place ask of me, rather than only what do I ask of it?

The question itself rearranges the room.

It shifts the center of gravity away from the human and back into the shared field of life. The chair turns slightly toward the light; the mind softens its edges. Suddenly, we are no longer the designers, but participants in an ongoing conversation.

It often begins with a small noticing. A leaf trembling though no wind is visible, the faintest shiver of movement where stillness should have been. The space around us isn't empty at all. It is alive with motion, with responsiveness, as if the air itself were thinking.

The old masters eventually gave this aliveness a name, but we feel it first in the body, before the mind can label it. The way a room holds its breath after laughter. The warmth of sunlight pooling against your chest. The current that moves between your hand and the bark of a tree when you pause long enough to really touch.

In the language of Feng Shui, everything is interdependent. The wall remembers the wind that dried its clay. The table holds a story of the forest the tree once belonged to. Even the birds who nest in your eaves engage in your home's design, drawing invisible lines of relationship between your life and theirs.

This way of understanding Feng Shui does not lean on superstition. It rests on the recognition of a shared field. It's the ecology of perception, how awareness itself rearranges the world.

When we pay attention to the way wind and water move, when we let them teach us how to live, we begin to remember what the ancients never forgot: that home is not where we withdraw from the world, but where we meet it most intimately.

Water itself is a master. It sculpts not by force but by persistence. It teaches that even in scarcity, flow can continue; seeping, spiraling, finding another way through. It gathers what the land offers, carries what it must, and rests where it can.

Perhaps our task is to live the same way. To flow without domination, to rest without forgetting movement, and to release structures that constrain life, making room for those that invite it.

When the wind stirs the trees, and the birds rise, when water catches light as it drifts downstream, this, too, is Feng Shui. It's not something we only apply to our homes, but something we remember in our bodies. The house becomes an echo of the landscape that shaped us.

This is where Feng Shui begins, not as a system, but as a way of sensing. Before we rearrange furniture or consult charts, we turn our attention to the smallest signal. The subtle shift in a room's mood. The change in the air when a door opens. The soft pull toward a place that feels right. How the world around you offers guidance without a word.

CHAPTER TWO

QI, THE BREATH BETWEEN ALL THINGS

What we sensed in the previous chapter now asks to be named. Qi is the subtle shimmering presence that moves between all things. It is not a metaphor. It is the field of relationships itself, the responsive consciousness that lives within wind, within water, within our breath. The ancients named it life energy, because they felt what we have forgotten, that everything we perceive is alive enough to respond.

Modern physics occasionally brushes against this knowing. Physicists have noticed that light behaves differently when observed, as if photons register attention, as if the smallest building blocks of the cosmos know when they are being seen. The world does not exist as inert matter waiting for us to act upon it; it arises in relationship, in mutual awareness.

Qi is that relational awareness. It is the intelligence of connection.

We feel Qi before we believe it exists. In the tension after anger leaves a room. In the way a forest seems to rest differently after rain. In the way a hawk locks onto a rising current of air and suddenly ascends without effort.

There are moments when the environment itself feels thick with meaning, as if we have walked into a conversation already underway. The kind that happens without words: roots speaking through soil, tides answering moonlight, a person softening when the wind ebbs.

If Qi lies beneath the unseen conversation, birds are its visible grammar. Watch their wings as they translate the invisible into motion, riding the breath of energy the wind already understands.

Qi is the medium that makes perception possible. It is what allows wind to sculpt sand. It is what allows birds to read invisible pathways across continents. It is what allows us to sense when a room is off before we notice anything out of place.

We do not learn Qi. We remember it. We have known this since we first had bodies. To sense Qi again is to soften. To notice that the space between things is not empty, but responsive, alive, listening back.

The ancients were not trying to manipulate energy. They were practicing coherence with it.

They understood that every placement, every angle, every threshold was a small act of communication, of respect, of empathy, of harmony.

As we begin again and learn to feel Qi beneath our feet and through the walls of our homes, we are not adding anything new to our understanding. We are returning to the truth that breath, perception, and place are braided from the same fabric.

This chapter is the first doorway.

QI — A WORKING DEFINITION

Qi is the living field of relationship that moves between all things — the subtle, conscious aliveness that arises through connection itself. Everything participates in Qi: wind, water, light, stone, animal, and human. Qi is not a force we control, but an intelligence we join through attention, reciprocity, and presence.

Before we move things around, we learn to feel again. Before we change the space, we let the space change us.

REFLECTION: THE LIVING SPACE BETWEEN

Sit somewhere simple: a chair, a patch of floor, the edge of a bed. Let your body settle into stillness.

Without effort, begin to notice the space *between* things: the air between your body and the wall, the hum between sounds, the slight drift of temperature, the quality of quiet that holds you.

Let your attention rest not on the objects of the room, but on the field in which they sit, the invisible fabric that touches everything.

As you soften your gaze, feel for that faint shimmer of aliveness, as if the room itself is aware of your presence. As if the space is the one noticing you. This is not imagination. This is the nervous system remembering how to listen.

Stay until you sense that the environment has shifted in response, even subtly, the way a forest rearranges its silence when an animal steps into it. Let that awareness move through you like a slight warmth, an exhale.

You are not sensing Qi from the outside. You are rejoining the relationship you never actually left. When you rise, do so with the gentleness of someone leaving a conversation that continues even in your absence.

CHAPTER THREE

THE YIN AND THE YANG OF FLIGHT

The hawk climbs in widening circles, every spiral a conversation between gravity and grace.

The air lifts, then releases. The body responds, never forcing, never resisting. Beneath the apparent power of flight lies deep surrender.

And below, a sparrow darts through reeds, all pulse and quicksilver. Its wings blur, the air trembling with vibration. Where the hawk trusts distance, the sparrow trusts immediacy.

One rides the thermal. One rides its own heartbeat.

Both express the same principle. Life is sustained by alternation between the still and the swift, the yielding and the assertive, the inhale and the exhale of motion.

Watch the birds. There is a moment in every flight when effort disappears. Wings fold slightly, muscles soften, and the bird rides what cannot be seen, the invisible hands of air rising from warmed ground. That is the moment of perfect balance.

Before this balance had a name, the world intoned its pattern. Light met shadow, warmth yielded to coolness, and wind carried both through the same valley. The ancients called this rhythm **Yin** and **Yang**, two aspects of one breath, endlessly transforming into each other.

Yin *is the receptive, the yielding, the inward.* The still pool that gathers light. The soft curve that holds.

Yang *is the active, the expressive, the outward.* The sun that rises. The pulse that expands.

Neither exists without the other. Neither is superior. Both are necessary.

Even in the moment of fullness lies the seed of decline. Even in the deepest rest lies the quiet inclination to rise. Balance, then, is not a frozen symmetry but a living conversation, the ceaseless exchange between stillness and motion, darkness and flame, gravity and grace.

In the Taoist symbol, the *Taijitu*, each swirl holds a drop of its opposite, reminding us that transformation is constant. Yin becomes Yang as night softens toward dawn; Yang becomes Yin as the day exhales into dusk. All movement, whether of seasons, of tides, or of wings, arises from this dialogue.

Nature knows this conversation.

Day yields to night. Rivers surge and then slow into pools. Even the heart, our inner house of Qi, contracts and releases, carrying the intelligence of balance into every breath.

The birds remind us that flight is not the conquest of air, but a relationship with it. The hawk rises because the thermal rises first. The sparrow lands because the wind has quieted. Between the two lies the wisdom of timing, knowing when to move and when to be carried.

Feng Shui teaches the same pattern. A space breathes when movement alternates with rest, when open areas are balanced by enclosure, and brightness is softened by shadow. What is true in the sky is true in the home, and in the heart.

The next time a bird crosses your path, a quick dart of motion, a steady glide overhead, watch not its wings, but the air around it. There, in the invisible play between resistance and release, is the oldest teaching of all. **Balance is not achieved by control, but by the ongoing conversation between things.**

PRACTICE: THE INHALE, THE EXHALE, THE WINGBEAT WITHIN

Sit or stand somewhere comfortable.

Let your shoulders soften, as if you were a bird folding its wings for a moment of rest.

Begin with the breath.

Without changing anything, notice your inhale. Feel it arrive on its own, the way air rises beneath a hawk.

Then notice your exhale, how it leaves without effort, like a sparrow settling into reeds.

Stay with the rhythm in your chest for a minute or two. Inhale, let your chest rise. Exhale, and release.

This is the simplest version of Yin and Yang.

Feel the pulse beneath the breath. When your breathing has softened, gently place two fingers on a pulse point: your wrist, your neck, or the spot just beside your heart.

Don't search for the beat. Wait for it.

Feel the steady alternation between contraction and expansion, between effort and rest.

Each pulse is its own small wingbeat, carrying you forward.

Sense the balance inside you. Let breath and heartbeat overlap in your awareness. The slow wave of air, the quick river of blood. Notice how they work together. One rising, one pulsing, one spacious, one rhythmic. Yin carried by Yang, Yang softened by Yin.

This is your internal flight pattern. The same balance that lifts a bird lives here, quietly, reliably.

Close with a simple acknowledgment. Place a hand over your chest and whisper inwardly: *"As above, so within. May I move with balance."*

Then return to your day, carrying that small harmony with you, a reminder that the body itself is a sky where balance is continually learned.

As above, so within. The same currents that lift a wing are present in us, quieter, smaller, but just as essential. When we understand balance in the sky, we are ready to recognize it in the body.

CHAPTER FOUR

HOMEOSTASIS - THE ART OF BALANCE

The same rhythm that carries a hawk on a thermal resonates through us and through all phenomena as effort and ease, gathering and release, motion and stillness.

Watch the tide. Even when seemingly tranquil, the water is never motionless. Molecules drift, eddies curl, the whole body of the sea surging and retreating under the pull of the moon. The same pulse lives in the body. Blood tides gush as the heart beats in its own lunar rhythm while the lungs inspire and exhale. Beneath the skin, a thousand exchanges unfold. Heat and cool, tension and release, contraction and expansion; all reveal the body's silent diplomacy between opposing forces.

This is the living conversation of Yin and Yang.

The body does not seek balance in perfect stillness. It seeks dynamic equilibrium, a center that moves. In biology, we call it homeostasis, the process of constant, intelligent adjustment. When heat builds, pores open. When cold settles, muscles draw inward. Heartbeat, breath rate, hormones. All shift in precise counterpoint.

We often speak of balance as something to find, a point of perfect poise that, once reached, will not waver. But the living world teaches otherwise. Stillness is not the opposite of movement, but its completion, the quiet in which direction clarifies. Motion, in turn, is not chaos, but the expression of stillness finding form. Day opens, night closes. The hawk circles on a thermal because the air is steady enough to sustain its lift. A seed bursts through the soil only after light penetrates and warms the soil after the cold, long darkness of waiting.

In the practice of Feng Shui, we arrange for this conversation. The still Yin corners that gather calm and the bright Yang rooms that invite riotous banter. A home that hums with life will also contain places of rest, shadows where the senses can soften. Without these, movement becomes agitation. Without movement, peace becomes stagnation.

There are times to open every window, to invite the world in with song and color. And there are times to draw the curtains, to let the air still and the light fade. Both are necessary for wholeness. Stillness asks for faith that life continues even when unseen, that the field beneath snow still dreams of green. Motion asks for courage, to act before knowing all the answers, to rise into uncertainty like wings meeting air.

Every living thing relies on this rhythm of expansion and contraction, rest and activity, night and day, inward and outward motion. These cycles regulate forests, tides, animal migrations, hormones, and metabolism. We forget this at our peril, for nothing in nature thrives by pushing in only one direction.

Our days lean too long toward Yang. Constant expansion, illumination, the bright hum of doing. But without Yin, without the pause, the shadow, and the still air, our wings tire. We fall out of rhythm with the Qi that sustains us.

Because we live in a culture that prizes Yang, action, productivity, and brightness, we often treat Yin as absence. Stillness becomes laziness. Rest becomes indulgence. Quiet becomes unproductive.

A bird pauses on a branch not because it is idle, but because stillness is part of flight.

When our lives become too Yang, too driven, bright, full, and fast, we lose the capacity to receive. When they are too Yin, too quiet, withdrawn, and stagnant, we lose the energy to participate. Balance emerges not as a 50/50 split, but as responsiveness. The body knows when it needs restoration. The spirit knows when it needs action.

When we forget the body's own Feng Shui, when we push without pause, or retreat without renewal, we lose our inner orientation. Thoughts spiral. Breath contracts. Muscles tense. The flow of Qi narrows to a trickle. Yet even then, the body remembers how to return. One slow breath, one long exhale, one loosening of the jaw, and already, the tide begins to turn.

To live in harmony with our bodies is to live as nature does: adjusting, yielding, recalibrating, returning. To honor this rhythm is to stop dividing your life into what counts and what doesn't, to see the pause as sacred, the action as prayer. To trust that the silence of the inner pause allows the inner wisdom of right action to emerge. Equilibrium is not a state to achieve, but a relationship to maintain. The body flowing with the rhythm of life, not against it.

PRACTICE: YOUR INNER LANDSCAPE

Close your eyes for a breath or two and imagine your body as a living terrain.

Where are the mountains of tension, the places that feel tight, braced, or lifted?

Where are the valleys of ease, the areas that feel soft, grounded, or open?

Where is the wind moving freely, the parts of the body where breath or warmth circulates without effort, and where has it stalled or grown still?

Let your attention wander gently, as if walking through familiar land. You are not trying to repair or control anything. You are only trying to recognize the shifting weather of your inner world.

Notice what is warm. Notice what is cool. Notice what wants to rise. Notice what wants to rest.

Yin and Yang are not opposites here. They are companions.

What might be asking for attention? Trust what you find. Allow your body to remember the way back to balance.

CHAPTER FIVE

THE FIVE ELEMENTS AS EARTH'S VERBS

From rhythm, form arises.

The dialogue of Yin and Yang becomes visible in the elements — water, wood, fire, earth, and metal — the cosmic dance of Qi made tangible.

What moves unseen through the air now takes shape in the living world. Water begins the story, gathering what is scattered. Wood rises from its depths toward light. Fire leaps, transforms, and releases. Earth receives and metabolizes what remains. Metal, last to form, distills clarity from what has passed. It is the refinement of experience itself.

Water — Strength in Softness, Power in Change

It was summer in the Grand Canyon, and the sun had painted the walls in impossible colors: rust, saffron, cinnabar, gold. Light didn't simply fall onto the rock there. It *inhabited* it. The canyon glowed from the inside out, as if the stone itself remembered every sunrise that had ever touched it, every river that had ever worn its way through its ribs.

Floating on the raft in still water, there were stretches where no one spoke. The silence wasn't an absence. It was an invitation to sink inward, a surface smooth enough for reflection both literal and felt. Even the canyon walls seemed to lean closer, listening with us. This is what Qi feels like in its water form, a receptivity so deep it becomes intelligence, a knowing that moves beneath words the way currents move beneath calm.

Water remembers. It holds history the way canyon walls hold shadow. It carves stone as the river strengthens. Just as often, it yields, flowing around obstacles, patient enough to return later in another form. Liquid, solid, or vapor, water is always becoming itself again, shifting states without ever losing its essence.

The water-carved canyon teaches us that memory is not static. It is erosion, a slow changing, a patient re-sculpting. Not erasing, but reforming. Likewise, what we remember reshapes itself over time, taking on the contours of life that has passed through it. Memory takes the shape of the inner weather that holds it. Sometimes clear, sometimes turbulent, sometimes frozen, sometimes dispersed into a fine mist of feeling. It can harden under fear, soften under love, evaporate under distance, or return unexpectedly as a sudden emotional downpour.

In the Grand Canyon, we float inside a memory so ancient it makes the human story feel like a brief flicker of attention in a much larger consciousness. Even the mirrored surface around us, those moments when the river turned glass-like, offered reflection not just of cliffs and sky, but of the quiet interior places we rarely see. Water doesn't simply keep the past. It shows us how the past keeps changing, how it moves through us in different emotional states, each one revealing a different truth.

Later, at Crystal Rapid, water revealed her other face. Not a gentle carrier but a force. The kind of force that does not negotiate. The type that requires surrender if you want to live through her. The raft dropped, the world turned white, and there was that moment where time became pure sensation. One boat flipped, dumping its occupants into the churn. Panic tore through the group like lightning. And then, just as quickly, instinct carried us. We pulled our friends, one by one, from the water. And when it was over, the river kept moving, utterly unchanged, utterly herself. Life-giving, life-taking, life-continuing.

Water teaches that surrender is not weakness. It is alignment with what is larger than will.

In Feng Shui, water is associated not with control, but with depth, with the unseen currents that shape us long before form appears. It is linked to the spiritual life not because it floats above the world, but because it runs beneath it. Water is the keeper of memory, the medium of remembering, the mystery that connects what has been to what is becoming.

Water's memory is the memory of the body. Water's intuition is the intuition of the Earth.

When we learn from water, we learn to soften without losing strength. We learn to change shape without losing center. We learn to remain connected to what came before while flowing toward what comes next.

Water is not passive. Water is relentless, alive, aware. It teaches that the path is not taken by force, but by insight, aligning yourself with the emotional currents within and the larger currents beyond, letting both guide the way forward.

And in this way, water is the first verb. The first movement of the world. The element that teaches us that there is no final destination, but a continuous becoming.

REFLECTION: THE FLOW OF MEMORY

Think of a memory that once felt solid in you. How has it softened, deepened, or taken on a new shape with time, the way water reshapes stone or a river returns in another season?

What changed in you that allowed it to shift? And what does this evolution reveal about the fluidity of your own understanding of memory?

Wood — The First Reaching

Spring in the Colorado foothills never arrives all at once. It comes in increments, in the slow unfreezing of creek edges, in that first startling greening of grass on the hillsides, in the way the ponderosas begin to smell sweeter as the sun climbs higher in the sky.

Before the leaves return, there is sound.

The mountain chickadees announce it first. Their voices cut the winter silence like a small bell, not loud, but unmistakably alive. One day, you realize that they are singing again. The air has loosened. The world has tilted back toward growth.

In Feng Shui, wood represents the movement toward expansion. Not the static state of being green, but the impulse to reach. The rising sap. The leaning toward light. The desire to live.

Birds feel this first. They return, they choose, they build. Not because the calendar says spring, but because the land tells them it is time.

In this way, Wood teaches us that growth is not a private act. It is always relational. It requires listening.

But Wood is not only the spring impulse. The Ponderosa teaches the other half. Wood is also memory. Each tree ring is a record of drought, of wet years, of lightning strikes survived. The trunk itself becomes a tablet of experience, written in slow increments of cellulose and sunlight.

And when a tree falls, its work is not done.

A fallen ponderosa becomes a world unto itself, a habitat for insects, a slow release of minerals, a nurse log that feeds the next generation. That is Wood, too. Not failure. Continuation.

Wood is the verb that stretches across the entire arc of life. Reaching. Growing. Thickening. Aging. Giving back.

When we align with Wood in our homes and bodies, we are aligning with this wisdom. Expansion without memory is unsustainable, but memory without new reaching becomes stagnation.

Qi moves through Wood as a creative impulse **and** as ancestral knowing. It rises, yes, but it also roots. There is no separation. The chickadee's spring song and the elder tree letting itself soften into the soil are part of the same cycle. One beginning implies a hundred endings before it. One ending is the nutrient that enables thousands of beginnings.

This is how Wood holds Feng Shui: it teaches us to grow *in relationship*, not in domination.

Growth that listens. Growth that remembers. Growth that feeds what comes after.

REFLECTION: THE NURSE LOG

Think of an ending in your life that felt like a loss or a failure. How did it eventually become soil for something new? A shift in direction, a new relationship, or a deeper understanding?

What grew from that ending that could not have grown without it?

Fire — The Intimate Flame

After a day on the trail, the light thinned to honey, and the foothills went quiet except for the faint crunch of twigs where unseen deer moved gently through the understory, the forest adjusting itself toward night. We cleared a small circle beneath open ponderosa, the bark rising in plates that smelled of warm vanilla where the sun had touched them all afternoon. A match, a whisper of dried grass, and then ember becoming tongue, becoming flame. Small at first, almost shy, then steady, then certain. We leaned into the light and warmth without speaking. The fire spoke in crackles and low vowels, a language older than words, drawing our attention the way the moon draws water.

Flames do what rivers do, only faster. They find a path. They move toward what feeds them. They turn matter into light and warmth, then into ash that becomes soil that will feed something else. In Feng Shui, fire is the verb of transformation. But here, in camp

tonight, it becomes another verb entirely. One of connection and belonging. Smoke threading our hair, heat loosening the day from our shoulders, sparks lifting into the dusk like tiny migrating stars.

Somewhere in the dark of the pines, a western tanager had gone still, its daytime blaze folded into feathered night. In daylight, it is a flare among needles, a bright echo of midday sun. At dusk, it is the memory of fire held close. The bird is flame in one register, ember in another. We are the same, bright sometimes, banked at others, carrying heat as a way to keep company with the world.

Fire teaches tenderness first. Tending is the opposite of conquest. We feed. We watch. We listen.

And yet inside the banked embers, there is also initiation, the quiet threshold where a stick becomes coal that becomes glow that becomes the possibility of a meal at dusk. If lightning is Fire's shout, the campfire is its vow. It says," Stay awhile. Be porous. Share warmth. Speak softly enough to hear the night answer."

Qi in its fire form is presence, attention that warms what it touches without consuming it. The more fully we attend, the steadier the flame. When attention fragments, the fire sputters. When attention returns, flame gathers itself and the circle brightens again. This is how rooms feel when care has lived there. This is how conversations become hearth. When presence meets presence, warmth accumulates, and something between us begins to glow with its own life.

Fire's counsel is simple. Keep the flame sized to the moment, feed it with what you truly have, let it go to ash when its work is done.

Warmth is a way of arranging love.

REFLECTION: RECEIVING AND OFFERING THE FLAME

Consider a moment when someone warmed your life with their presence.

What ember did they offer you? Kindness? Attention? Patience? How might you offer a similar flame to someone who needs it now?

Earth — The Hands That Hold

In my own garden, kneeling among tomatoes and basil and bee balm, the world narrows and widens at the same time. My hands sink into soil still cool from the night, and the weight of it changes my breathing. The soil is not just dirt. It is memory ground finely enough to hold roots, water, nitrogen, and hope. When I press my palms into it, my body drops an octave lower, as if the Earth itself is saying, "*You can rest here.*"

Earth is the element of metabolizing, turning experience into nourishment.

It takes what has been, the fallen pine needles, the forgotten petals, and last season's compost and turns it into something that can feed life again. Time thickens in the soil, where the countless unseen lives of microbes, mycelium, and the creatures of decomposition work in quiet collaboration. Nothing is wasted. Nothing is rejected. Everything is received.

Some days I simply sit there with my hands open, letting soil run through my fingers like a slow hourglass. This settles me. In Feng Shui, Earth corresponds with the center. Not the

center as a pedestal, but the center as a table. The place where things can gather. Where the right relationships can form.

Earth is the quiet intelligence of arrangement, not control, but coherence. The same instinct that orders roots and stones into an ecosystem invites us to arrange our inner world so life can move through it with less resistance.

Here, this belongs next to that. Shade plants here. Sun lovers there. Clay is softened with compost. Paths wander through. There's a home for bees, a corridor for worms, a space for roots to negotiate.

Soil knows how to hold many lives at once.

And this is what Earth asks of us: to be a ground where complexity can come to rest without collapsing. To be steady enough that emotion can settle. To be patient enough that meaning can aggregate. To be centered enough that other beings, the feathered, rooted, or human, can find a tiny moment of ease in our presence.

When I kneel and scatter the cooled embers of a campfire or a fireplace, Earth receives what Fire has become. When I tuck seeds into soil in spring, Earth receives potential without demanding outcome. When I bury kitchen scraps in the compost, Earth receives the ending of one form so another can begin.

Earth holds without needing to possess.

Qi in Earth is weight, stillness, and safety, but not stagnation. It is the fertile pause. The breath between growth and letting go.

To honor Earth in practice is simple. Make places where life can settle. Make surfaces where life can land. Make space where everything unnecessary can drop away without fear.

Earth is the element that teaches us that belonging is what lets the world reorganize around life. This is what soil knows.

REFLECTION: BECOMING GROUND

Think of a time when someone needed steadiness more than answers. How did you offer, or how might you have offered, a place for them to settle, a ground where nothing had to be fixed immediately, only held? What would it feel like, even for a single moment, to be soil for someone else's becoming?

Metal — The Beauty of Letting Go

By late autumn, the field is mostly quiet. The meadowlarks have gone. The air has a thin, silver quality, as if all excess has drained from the world. The grasses stand brittle, seedheads sharp with frost. Everything is reduced to line, essence, structure. Metal lives here, not in the chill of the season, but in the clarity of the world made stark, one stripped of everything to its essential form.

A golden eagle circles high above the expanse, riding currents with patient precision. It does not flap or force. It waits until the exact right moment reveals itself, then moves. This is Metal's aerial intelligence, the discernment that arises when we lift above the noise and see the pattern clearly.

But another teacher lives at ground level. It's the winter sparrow, plain and nearly invisible until it moves. It picks seed by seed, one humble kernel at a time. It shows the other face of Metal, the clarity that comes not from grand vision, but from exactness in the small.

Metal holds both scales at once. The high, broad view that simplifies by seeing the whole, and the close, quiet view that simplifies by noticing what actually matters.

Later at home in late autumn light, I feel that same thinning impulse in my rooms. It's the desire to make space. To let the air move through the house without obstruction. I put my hand on a stack of papers that hasn't been touched in months, and without forcing anything, the mind simply knows. This can go. The clarity arrives before the story about it. This is how Qi moves in Metal: swift, clean, without drama. Letting go doesn't feel like loss, it feels like alignment.

In Feng Shui, Metal governs refinement, distillation, and decision. Not a decision with a hard edge, but a decision with maturity, the ability to release the nonessential so that what remains can ring true. Metal is the tone a bell makes when shape and density are in perfect proportion. It is the unburdened shelf with one beloved bowl placed just right. It is the winter sky that reveals the mountain's actual bones.

Metal teaches that clarity is a kindness to ourselves, to others, to place.

Not everything that enters our lives is meant to stay. Not every thought deserves a shrine. Not every possession is meant to be carried forward.

When we align with Metal, we refine with tenderness rather than scarcity. We honor the whole arc. Water remembers. Wood reaches. Fire warms. Earth integrates. Then Metal pares away what no longer serves so that the cycle can begin again unencumbered.

The gift of Metal is the exhale that makes room for the next inhale. This is how balance continues. Not by accumulation, but by releasing what cannot sing.

PRACTICE: ONE GENTLE CLEARING

Choose one tiny area: a single shelf, a drawer, a surface. Clear it slowly, not to empty it, but to restore breath. Ask: *What still belongs in relationship with me? What has completed its season?*

Let intuition answer, not obligation. When you finish, touch the space. Feel the lightness.

CHAPTER SIX

THE WORLD AS A CONVERSATION

Before we invented the word Qi or named the five elements, we understood something simpler. The world was speaking, and we were part of its speech. Wind moved through grasses, water carved its patient paths, and birds read the invisible and placed their nests accordingly. Our bodies registered these changes long before we tried to interpret them.

Qi is not an abstraction but the felt energy between things: warmth rising, shadows lengthening, currents of air slipping around our skin. Yin and Yang describe how that energy moves. Gathering and releasing, brightening and dimming, resting and rising. The five elements illustrate the qualities of that movement in the world. Water remembering and yielding. Wood reaching toward light. Fire gathering warmth and belonging. Earth holding and metabolizing. Metal clarifying and letting go. They are not separate forces but recurring verbs the Earth speaks through.

Our perception is the bridge that connects us to these patterns. To notice light, sound, slope, or breeze is to step back into a relationship with the living field. When we open a window because the room feels heavy, follow an instinct to turn a chair toward the morning sun, or feel steadier with our back to a solid wall, we are already in conversation with Qi. The world offers signals. We respond. A home placed on a hillside, a path bent by wind, a bird choosing where to land, each gesture is part of an ongoing exchange.

This is the root of Feng Shui. It is not a system we impose on the land, but a way of noticing how the land already arranges itself, how streams find their course, how trees lean into light, or how birds choose the right branch. When we attend to Qi, to elemental qualities, to the quiet intelligence of the living world, we remember that we are not separate observers. We are participants in a broader conversation that surrounds and sustains us.

Seen this way, Feng Shui becomes very simple. It is the practice of paying attention to what is already happening and aligning ourselves with it. It asks, again and again: *What does this place ask of me, as much as what do I ask of it?* Our homes, our bodies, and the wider landscape all answer in their own dialects of ease and discomfort, flow and friction, brightness and rest.

From here, the work of placing homes, tending space, and living with reciprocity begins. But all of it rests on this simple truth. The world is speaking. We are meant to listen and to let our choices be our way of gently speaking back.

REFLECTION / PRACTICE: A SMALL CONVERSATION WITH PLACE

Choose one spot you spend time in. A room, a desk, a corner by a window.

Stand or sit there quietly for a moment.

Ask, inwardly: *What is already happening here? Where does the light want to fall? Where does the air want to move? Where does my body feel most at ease?*

Let your attention drift over the space the way the wind moves over a field. Notice any slight tug of intuition. A chair that wants to turn, an object that wants to be cleared, a plant that wants more light, or a surface that wants to be empty.

Make one small change as a response. Not to perfect the space, but to acknowledge the conversation.

Feel how the room, and your body within it, subtly shifts. This is Feng Shui at its root. Paying attention, answering kindly, and letting the world and the self meet each other halfway.

PART TWO
THE SACRED GEOGRAPHY OF PLACE

Part One has reminded us that the world is not silent nor separate from us. It has a language, and we are capable of hearing it again. When we listen long enough, patterns begin to reveal themselves: where light prefers to fall, how water shapes a valley, the quiet certainty with which birds choose their resting places. These patterns are not abstractions. They are the geography of the living Earth.

Part Two turns toward that geography, the directions, orientations, and relationships that arise naturally from the land, and explores how the Bagua (an energy map that identifies areas associated with different life aspects) grew from these same ways of seeing.

CHAPTER SEVEN

WHERE THE BIRDS WOULD BUILD

The hummingbird nest was so small we would have never seen it if we hadn't watched her movements first.

Broad-tailed hummingbirds move like flecks of green iridescent light, quick flashes, here, then gone. But that summer, I began to notice she always vanished into the same green pocket of the crabapple, just five feet off the ground. Only then did the nest become visible, but only through attention, noticing the pattern before the object. The nest itself was the size of a walnut shell, held together with spider silk, lichen, grass, bits of moss, and threads finer than hair. Not ornament. Not display. Almost invisible unless you already knew it existed.

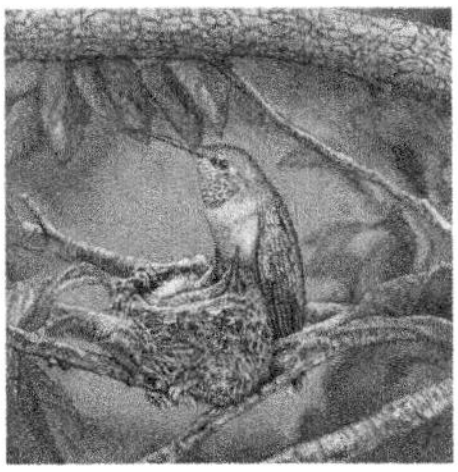

A nest is never an accident. She had chosen a place where morning sun filtered in just gently enough to warm without overexposing, where leaves broke the wind, where branches offered both cradle and concealment. Invisible, but attended to. We watched as she fed, hovered, rested, turned. She raised two young that season, two tiny new beings woven into the weft of this one small tree. When we watched those nestlings finally rise and leave the branch, it felt like witnessing a sentence complete itself. A grammar of air. A syntax of relationship.

Birds build as if the world is alive and responsive, not inert. They build as if the elements are collaborators, not obstacles to overcome. There is a kind of holy intelligence in that. Wind is not "weather" to a bird. It gives birth to architecture and design.

No blueprint. Only attunement.

This is what Feng Shui actually teaches first, not where to place an object or a chair, but how to read the currents that already exist. Because placement is only meaningful if it contributes to the flow of life, rather than resisting it.

And birds know this.

They know where shelter actually is. Not a hypothetical shelter. Not a symmetrical shelter. Not a pretty shelter. Lived shelter. They build in conversation with the forces that shaped the land long before humans ever spoke words like *Feng* and *Shui*. There is a humility in that, to build in response.

Often, when I sit inside my home, I think about that nest. How much of our design is about "expressing identity" or "achieving aesthetic" rather than belonging to currents larger than ourselves? How often do we choose what is visually pleasing over what is wise? How often do we try to command rather than align?

Birds remind us that a home is not a statement; it is a relationship. The hummingbird didn't build high for prestige. She built close to the heart of the tree. Near warmth. Where wind wouldn't tear and leaves would hold. She built within reciprocity, not superiority.

What if the purpose of shelter was not to shut the world out but to create a permeable membrane through which the world could still speak? What if safety were not a barricade, but collaboration? Maybe this is the meaning of returning home to Feng Shui at this time. To learn again to site, arrange and dwell in our homes the way birds do, with sensitivity rather than will.

Maybe this is what a house that breathes starts with. Not the things we put in it, but the attention we are willing to offer it. The birds have not forgotten how to choose the right relationship with place. They are still teaching the rest of us, if we are willing to understand.

CHAPTER EIGHT

WHERE THE ANCIENTS WOULD BUILD - THE FOUR CELESTIAL ANIMALS

Before there were compasses or maps, there was only the body reading the land. People stood still and listened to the hum of wind through grass, the long breath of a valley, the bright pulse of a spring emerging from stone. They watched the way mist gathered and released, how morning light warmed one slope but not another. Every feature was a gesture, every shadow a word.

To choose a place to live was to enter a conversation. The earliest Feng Shui masters were not architects or mystics, but listeners. They were those who could feel the Earth's pulse beneath their feet. They sensed where energy flowed freely, where it pooled and lingered, where it turned turbulent or still. The Chinese originally called this practice ***kan yu***, "to observe heaven and earth," and later called it Feng Shui. It was less about prediction than discernment.

Out of this intimacy came the language of the Four Celestial Animals, not myth, but metaphor born of observation. They were ways of describing how a good landscape holds and protects life, much as branches cup a bird's nest or a valley shelters a stream.

To the south, the ancients saw the Red Phoenix, wings spread toward the open sky, where light and possibility expanded. This was the aspect of vision, a clear view before the home, allowing Qi to enter and move freely.

To the north, they placed the Black Tortoise, steady and enduring, the shape of a mountain or rise of land that gave protection to the back. It was the unseen strength, the memory of ancestors, the slow accumulation of wisdom and shelter.

On the east, the Azure Dragon coiled, vital and alive, its form mirrored by flowing water or soft rising terrain. This was the force of growth, the stirring energy of beginnings, the breath of dawn that animates.

To the west, the White Tiger crouched, alert, guarding, defined by precise edges and discernment. It was not a symbol of danger but of balance, ensuring that openness never became exposure.

Together, these four became the anatomy of place, how the land itself cradled life. When the mountain rose behind, when water curved before, when the hills flanked gently on either side, the site was said to be well-protected and to breathe well. A person living there would thrive, not because of magic, but because the land's pattern aligned with the body's own sense of ease.

This was Feng Shui before it had a name, before formulas and grids, when instinct and reverence guided the hand. It was, in essence, the art of listening and belonging.

Today, many of us no longer build in the open country. We rely on permits and blueprints, not intuition. Yet the Earth's anatomy remains. Hills and hollows, shadows and wind currents still shape how Qi moves through our lives. To remember the Four Celestial

Animals is to remember that every place has a posture, and our well-being depends on recognizing it.

Even now, when I watch a bird test the wind before building a nest, I think of those early masters, reading the unseen through the visible, choosing their ground not by power, but by relationship. The world still teaches this if we are willing to lower our arrogance and pay attention.

CHAPTER NINE

THE ANCIENT COURTYARD AND THE LIVING NEST

Before architecture became ambition, it was an act of listening, a way of placing one's ear against the world and building in response to what it whispered. The arrangement and placement of buildings in a community mirrored a cosmological understanding that was emerging alongside them, shared ways of reading the land and the seasons. Buildings corresponded to mountains, walls to protective hills, and the paths threading through them to rivers guiding qi through the landscape.

The ancient Chinese *siheyuan,* the traditional courtyard home, was shaped by this kind of listening. Its builders understood that a house does not stand *on* the land but exists in harmony *with* it, answering the movements of sun, wind, and season the way a body answers breath.

"Traditional Chinese Siheyuan Courtyard" (https://skfb.ly/prMRZ) by andertan is licensed under Creative Commons Attribution (http://creativecommons.org/licenses/by/4.0/).

A home turned inward, with four buildings embracing a rectangle of open sky, formed a small world of calm within its walls. It was a human nest, open to light and weather, yet held in quiet protection. The courtyard lay at the center, not as an empty space, but as the living heart around which every room breathed. Here, architecture was not only spatial but cosmological. It was a way of aligning the human household with heaven above, earth below, and the relationships that knit people together.

A typical siheyuan rests on a north–south axis. The most honored building sits in the north, its entrance facing south, where winter sun can enter generously and cold northern winds are held at a respectful distance. This was the dwelling of the elders, those whose sage years had earned the warmest light. It was also the place where qi, carried by sunlight and softened breezes, could gather and remain. Here, timing, placement, and relationship converged: the sun's arc, a suitable position in the land, and the steady presence of the elders who held the family together. The north hall embodied this union, holding social order and natural forces in a single, sheltering gesture.

Along the eastern and western sides stretched the wings, balanced like outstretched arms, holding the rooms of married sons, children, and younger kin, their symmetry echoing the Confucian order that shaped family and society alike.

And at the southern edge, where sunlight is least abundant, a more modest building awaited guests or held those of lesser rank. Here dwelt the daughters-in-law, concubines, and servants. This was a gentle acknowledgment that even architecture conveys the epoch's hierarchy in the way it arranges space.

Even arrival was its own choreography. A gate in the southeastern corner opened not into the courtyard itself but toward a protective screen wall, a gentle turn meant to slow incoming wind, keep the home's accumulated energy from spilling outward, while giving the home privacy and inviting the visitor to slow their steps before entering.

Some siheyuan held a single courtyard. Others were layered several in sequence, each one a small universe with its own rhythm, sheltering generations of family.

The organization of these spaces was more than functional. It mirrored Confucian values, placing elders at the axis of honor and arranging all other rooms with symmetry meant to express balance, continuity, and respect. The outer walls protected the household like a cupped hand, but within, the courtyard gathered everyone into shared life. Its openness encourages conversations, play, meals, and the daily weaving of family.

Every room of the home touched the open center, receiving light and air. The materials of wood, tile, and brick were drawn from the land itself, making the home an extension of the earth it rested on. Often the courtyard carried its own pocket of nature: a flowering tree, a shallow pool that caught sky, a scatter of stones arranged with care. Here, the natural world was not outside the threshold but folded into everyday living.

I think of such courtyards when I remember the hummingbird's nest woven in the crook of our crabapple tree. So small it could vanish in the shelter of my palm, yet crafted with the same intimate logic. A structure built to meet a particular place, held together by spider silk, moss, and the patience of a creature who trusts the world enough to build with its offerings.

Her nest, too, was an inward-facing home. A circle open to the weather, open to light, open to the passing breezes that cooled summer mornings. No walls to keep the world out. Only boundaries that helped her young belong to it.

There is wisdom in both dwellings. The siheyuan and the hummingbird's nest teach us that shelter need not be separation. A home can hold its people gently while still letting wind wander through and letting sunlight find its way in.

To build, or to live, in this spirit is to ask simple, essential questions. **How does the day move here? Where does the air wish to flow? What arrangement of space allows life to thrive?**

We don't need a four-walled courtyard to find a place to listen. A window left open in the right season, a slant of afternoon light inviting itself across the floor, or a place where inside leans toward outside, are small courtyards of their own.

The hummingbird's nest lasted only a summer, yet what remains, that faint cup of silk and the hum of memory around its edges, reminds me of the old homes. Places where right dwelling is not just walls and roofs, but the space where the world is welcomed in, and life gathers itself around an open sky

THE MEASURE OF AUSPICE — UNDERSTANDING THE LU BAN RULER

Before modern measurements standardized the world, Chinese carpenters used a tool that carried both length and meaning. This was the **Lu Ban ruler**, named after the mythic master builder credited with bringing the first saws, squares, and plumb lines into human hands. To use the ruler was not only to measure wood; it was to align a home with fortune.

Unlike our familiar tape measures, the Lu Ban ruler held **two systems at once**. One was the ordinary scale of inches and feet (or in the ancient dimensions, *cun* and *chi*). The other was a repeating band of words: *wealth, prosperity, sickness, lawsuit, open flower, separate apart, heavenly virtue, death gate*. Each labeled segment was understood as auspicious or inauspicious. The carpenter's task was to cut doors, lintels, thresholds, and beds so that their dimensions fell within the benevolent intervals while avoiding the harmful ones.

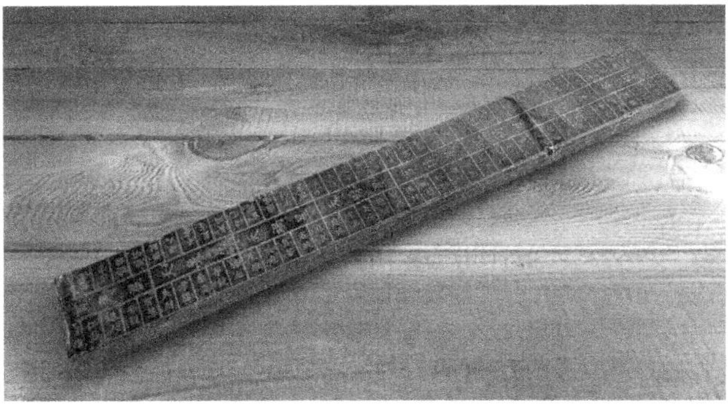

In practice, this turned carpentry into a quiet ritual, aligned with a pattern of blessing. A doorway was not simply sized to admit a body, but to welcome good fortune. Thresholds became places of care, that qi might cross them gently and not rush through or falter. A step riser was chosen so that no misfortune would befall the foot that climbed it. A bed platform was measured not just for comfort, but so that rest itself might be sheltered by favorable qi.

It is worth noting that there were several Lu Ban rulers, each for a different purpose: one for houses, one for furniture, one for tombs. Even in death, measure still mattered. Yet beneath the variations ran the same belief, that the spaces we shape also shape us, and that numbers can be tuned like strings to carry harmony.

Not everyone who used the Lu Ban ruler believed in its power. For many craftsmen, it was simply tradition, a way of honoring the lineage of builders before them. But tradition itself can be a form of listening, a willingness to let the old ways remind us that a home is more than shelter. It is a vessel for relationship, for continuity, for the quiet hope that what we build today might offer a blessing to the ones who will pass through its thresholds tomorrow.

In this sense, the Lu Ban ruler was not superstition so much as **a practice of intention,** a belief that dimensions can carry care, and that the shape of a doorway might echo a wish for wellbeing. It reminds us that measurement, at its most human, is never just about lengths of wood. It is about the unseen things we hope our homes will hold.

REFLECTION: OPENING

And perhaps the question now is not only how our ancestors built, or how a hummingbird shapes her nest, but how *we* might inhabit our own places with similar discernment. As you reach this point in this dialogue, you might turn your attention toward whatever space surrounds you and ask it quietly:

Where do you breathe?

Where does the light linger?

What small threshold invites the world in?

Modern life has taught us to prize enclosure, to seal our windows against noise and weather, to wrap ourselves in insulation and call it safety. But these older dwellings whisper a different story. Comfort is not born from shutting things out, but from discovering a right-sized openness, a way of letting the world enter in its gentler forms and letting ourselves find a place within the larger breathing around us.

So, you might look for the places in your life where enclosure has become a habit rather than a need.

Where could a door open for a moment?

Where might a curtain be drawn back?

Where could air or light be allowed to speak again?

Every threshold, after all, is an invitation. Every shaft of sunlight is its own quiet teacher. Every breeze, even the faintest one, reminds us that we are not sealed beings, but participants in a shared atmosphere.

You don't need a courtyard of carved wood and brick to practice this kind of belonging.

You need only a willingness to listen to the way your own walls meet the day, to the way the world touches your home, and the way your home touches you.

And if you respond, even once, to one small invitation of light or air, you join a lineage of builders, human and feathered, who understood that dwelling is not separation, but relationship. A practice of opening where we can, sheltering where we must, and letting life gather itself around its own patch of open sky.

CHAPTER TEN

THE BAGUA

Before it was drawn as a diagram, the bagua was felt as a rhythm. It was an energy map understood through experience, revealing how each direction carries a distinct quality of Qi, each shaping life in its own way. It reflected an understanding that life unfolds through pattern and through relationship held in balance.

Across cultures and climates, long before diagrams or doctrine, people were already gathering their homes around open centers as a convergent response to light, weather, the need for protection, and the human longing for both privacy and connection. The architecture of the siheyuan, the ancient Chinese courtyard home, embodied this knowing. Built around an open center, an earthly reflection of the heavens above, the courtyard gathered light, air, and conversation into a shared heart. Its rooms extended outward like petals around stillness, each oriented not by abstraction but by attention to sun, wind, season, and kinship. It was, in essence, a living atlas of belonging.

The Bagua did not create this impulse or invent the siheyuan, but gave it language, allowing an ancient way of dwelling to be consciously aligned with direction, season, and the movement of Qi. Nor did the siheyuan simply illustrate the Bagua. They evolved together, one as a lived form, the other as a symbolic memory, each helping the other remember how to hold a balance between heaven and earth. The bagua diagram gathered centuries of observation into a portable language, a way of carrying the intelligence of place.

As this understanding matured, builders began to align existing courtyard forms more deliberately with cosmological principles. They oriented gates and halls according to elemental and directional relationships. What had once been guided primarily by climate, kinship, and craft was gradually refined through Feng Shui, not imposed from outside, but named from within.

At the center was the Tai Chi, the still point where heaven and earth met. This was not empty space, but fullness held in quiet balance, a place where the family could stand beneath the open sky yet remain sheltered within the walls. The ancients understood that this center was the axis of all movement, the heart that allowed the house to breathe. To step into it was to be reminded that stability does not mean stasis, but the calm through which a life in motion flows.

Around that center, the eight directions unfolded, each a gesture of relationship between human and world. The Bagua captured how light enters from the south, how mountains protect to the north, and how dawn and dusk balance the day between them. It was a conversation between direction and meaning. Not an invention, but a noticing.

In the east, where the sun rose, they placed *Zhen*, the thunder that stirs beginnings, the vitality of growth.

To the south, *Li*, the fire of illumination, the sun's heart radiance that ripens what is growing.

To the west, *Dui*, the lake, a place of reflection and joy, where energy softens into completion.

To the north, *Kan*, the deep waters: mystery, rest, and endurance. Between them, the other four directions of *Xun* (wind), *Qian* (heaven), *Gen* (mountain), and *Kun* (earth) completed the square, balancing movement and repose, expansion and containment. Together they traced the rhythm of the world's breath.

To live within the Bagua was not to follow a prescription, but to dwell in awareness of the relationship between all things. The courtyard home mirrored the logic of the land around it, tracing light and shadow, openness and boundary. Its design acknowledged that human life depends on both exposure and refuge, clarity and depth. The Bagua simply named what the land already practiced. It was balance made visible.

Today, we often reduce the Bagua to a grid, a tool to overlay on floor plans. But its original meaning was fluid, responsive. It was the map of the house as a living organism, the mind as an open field, the world as a breathing pattern. The ancients did not use it to impose order. They used it to remember that harmony arises when we align ourselves with the greater flow.

At its heart, the Bagua reminds us that all forms, whether homes, bodies, relationships, or ecosystems, share one architecture: a center that holds, and directions that reach. It is the shape of reciprocity itself, showing us how life radiates outward and returns to stillness. To stand in our own courtyard, whether it is a garden, a room, or the space between breaths, is to enter that same geography. The center is still here, not out in the courtyard, but in the quiet place within us that remembers how to listen and how to step back into a relationship with the world that shaped it.

DIRECTION IS ALSO LANDSCAPE

The Bagua originated among people living in the Northern Hemisphere, where the sun arcs across the southern sky. Their elemental associations reflect the land that shaped their perception: the warmth of the south, the depth of the north, the rising vitality of the east, the softening completion of the west.

If you live in the Southern Hemisphere, the sun travels a different path; warmth comes from the north, and the qualities of light, season, and direction shift accordingly. And even within the same hemisphere, mountains, oceans, forests, and deserts all alter the flavor of direction. A southern exposure means something different beside a glacier than beside a sea. A western wind carries a different story in the Rockies than it does on the coast of New Zealand.

This is how the Bagua asks to be understood: not as a rigid template, but as a relationship with the land beneath your feet. The map is not universal; the *conversation* is.

Wherever you live, notice how your place behaves; how light enters, where warmth gathers, where wind rests or rises, what features protect, expose, soften, or amplify.

The Bagua lives in these observations first.

Optional Practice: Mapping the Directions Where You Live

Step outside or stand at a window in your home. Let your body turn slowly in a full circle. As you face each direction, ask:

- What does this direction offer here?
- Warmth? Shadow? Wind? Stillness? Rise? Retreat?
- What natural feature shapes it?
- A mountain, a city, a body of water, an open field?
- What quality does your body feel as you face it?
- Expansion? Grounding? Softening? Clarity?

You are not looking for the "right" answer. You are letting the land teach you its own Bagua. When you finish, pause at your personal center, that point from which all directions can be felt.

Let this be the place where your home's conversation begins.

BAGUA

The Bagua (pronounced bah-gwah) is an ancient Chinese framework used in Feng Shui to understand how energy moves through space. It describes a center, where balance is held, surrounded by eight directions, each associated with distinct qualities of life and Qi. These directions are traditionally expressed through eight simple symbols, or trigrams, that reflect natural forces such as heaven, earth, thunder, wind, water, fire, mountain, and lake.

CHAPTER ELEVEN

THE BAGUA OF A LIFE

The Bagua was never meant to merely map a floor plan. It was always a mirror, a way to see the patterns that connect the landscape of a home to the landscape of a soul. Just as wind and water move through the valleys of the earth, intention and attention move through the valleys of a life. Whether stretched across a plot of land, over the rooms of a home, or inward across the terrain of a life, the Bagua reveals repeating contours. Places of flow, places of stagnation, places asking for care. The pattern endures. It is we who move closer or farther from it. By adjusting the scale, we begin to see that the geography of our surroundings and the geography of our inner world are reflections cast from the same source.

Each direction, each aspect, speaks to a rhythm of being, and always, its opposite answers back. Balance doesn't live in the single note, but in the chord, the tension held between what we reach for and what we return to. To live the Bagua of life is to understand that every area of our being relies on its reflection of counterparts, that one cannot flourish without the other.

To the north lies Kan, the Water of Life that is the realm of career, purpose, and the flow of becoming. Its mirror is to the south, Li, the Fire of recognition. Not fame in the shallow sense, but illumination. How are we seen? How is our light shared? Without water's depth, fire burns out. Without fire's warmth, water grows cold and hidden. Together, they ask, "Can I move in the world with both direction and authenticity, allowing my gifts to shine while remaining rooted in what nourishes me?"

To the east, Zhen, the Thunder wood of new beginnings, rises. It represents our family, ancestry, and growth. Its partner, in the west, is Dui, the metallic distillation of our creativity, expression, and completion. Wood stretches outward while metal refines inward. Creation and refinement are two halves of the same motion. One reaching, one distilling. The lineage we inherit becomes the art we offer back. Our roots and our voice grow from the same soil.

To the northeast, Gen, the mountain, holds knowledge, reflection, and self-cultivation. Across the way, the southwest opens into partnership, relationship, and compassion. We cannot meet another deeply until we have met ourselves. Likewise, we only come to know ourselves fully through the mirror of others. Learning and loving are one breath, the inhalation and exhalation of understanding.

In the northwest, Qian, the realm of Heaven speaks of helpful people and mentors. They are the unseen hands that lift us, guide us, and open paths. Its complement, Xun in the southeast, is Wind and wealth, not merely material abundance, but the circulation of blessings, the giving and receiving that sustains life. When generosity moves through us, help arrives. When help arrives, generosity expands. Both are currencies of trust in the living world.

And at the center is Tai Chi, the Earth, the heart of stillness, where all these movements meet. It is the courtyard within, the breath between heartbeats, the pause between giving and receiving. Without the center, direction has no meaning. Without stillness, movement loses its grace.

To live the Bagua of a life is to trace the same architecture that orders wind and water. It is a pattern of reciprocity. It reminds us that our purpose flows toward visibility and then back to depth, that our roots rise into song and return to soil, that our learning folds into love and unfurls again as wisdom.

We are not separate from these forces. We are their continuation. When we honor both sides of every current, the inner and outer, self and other, our reaching and returning, life begins to breathe through us as it once breathed through the courtyard, the mountain, and the open sky.

And perhaps that is the quiet teaching of the Bagua. Wholeness is not perfection, but participation and negotiation, the grace of moving in rhythm with the circle that never ends.

CHAPTER TWELVE

PRACTICES FOR LIVING THE BAGUA

Before moving a single object in your home, begin with yourself. Feng Shui is not first about furniture or floor plans. It starts with awareness. The Bagua map, like any map, only reveals what you are ready to see.

Before there were diagrams, there were gestures. Before there were instructions, there was breath.

Feng Shui began not as a system of placement, but as a practice of perception, a way of noticing how life moves through us and around us. The circle of the Bagua is not just a grid to influence your home. It is a mirror to help you see where energy already flows, and where it waits to be invited back.

Each direction in the Bagua mirrors a landscape within the self, the inner terrain of purpose, wisdom, family, abundance, illumination, relationship, creativity, and legacy. These are not fixed categories but living climates. Their boundaries shift as we grow.

Before you look at where these energies lie in your home, pause to feel where they live in you. This is the practice of *inner arrangement,* of discovering the harmony or imbalance already present before seeking to correct it.

You may wish to move slowly, one direction at a time, reflecting on the questions offered for each direction. Notice which evoke ease and which stir restlessness. Both are invitations. This is not self-analysis. It is listening to the subtle weather of your own life.

When you have walked once around the circle within, the Bagua of your home will begin to speak differently. You may see that the cluttered corner reflects more than storage habits, or that a bright window opens toward a part of life that is thriving.

These reflections are not meant to be done all at once. You might follow them in the order of the compass, or open to the one that calls to you. Each is a threshold, an inner inquiry before you rearrange a single thing.

Sit first. Listen. Let your inner landscape reveal where harmony already lives and where care is needed. Then, when you move to touch the outer world, be it the chair, the lamp, or the open window, you will do so with the same sensitivity the early geomancers used to read the land.

Each direction offers its own rhythm. Stillness and flow. Root and branch. Light and reflection. Giving and return. Together, they form a breathing circle. They are the life within your home, your body, your work, and your relationships. Let these practices be less about arranging your space and more about remembering your place within the living pattern.

The circle begins at the North, where still water gathers and purpose waits beneath the surface.

NORTH — THE RIVER OF PURPOSE AND DEPTH

The North is the realm of water, where the surface stills but the current runs deep. It is the place of vocation, mystery, and inner listening. It's the long conversation between who we are and what life asks of us. To walk northward is to follow the sound beneath sound, the murmur of your own current returning to its source.

Reflect gently:

- **What work, visible or invisible, feels most like water moving through me?**
- **Where in my life have I mistaken stillness for stagnation, or motion for meaning?**
- **Can I trust the pauses as much as the surges?**

Water finds its way by yielding. It does not force direction. It senses. Purpose, too, flows best when we stop insisting and start listening. And when the river slows to a near stillness, reflection becomes the movement itself. The current deepens into silence, and what was once pursuit turns to understanding. This is the turning of water toward the mountain, the quiet ascent into wisdom.

NORTHEAST — THE QUIET ASCENT (WISDOM, REFLECTION, STILLNESS)

When water meets the mountain, motion becomes reflection. The North's deep current turns inward in the Northeast, rising into the thin, clear air where understanding gathers. Wisdom is not a destination but a climate. It arrives when the winds of thought calm. Like snow collecting on high ridges, insight is the slow work of stillness.

Reflect:

- **What have I learned that my mind knows but my body has not yet trusted?**
- **Where in my life am I asked to pause, not out of fatigue, but ripening?**
- **How might stillness itself be a form of participation?**

The wisdom of this direction hums beneath silence, preparing the world for spring.

From stillness, movement is born again.

EAST — THE BREATH OF RENEWAL (NEW BEGINNINGS, FAMILY, HEALTH)

At the edge of night, the first light stirs. Here, in the East, the pulse of life begins again with wood pushing upward, birdsong multiplying, and air tasting of green. This is the realm of beginnings, of the first deep breath after long dormancy. Renewal is not a return to what was, but a reaching toward what can be.

Reflect:

- **What is beginning to rise in me that I haven't yet named?**
- **What has been waiting, quietly, for the light?**
- **How do I nurture growth without rushing it?**

In the East, energy unfurls gently, not in haste. Like a bud trusting warmth, we learn that vitality is the courage to open. And where life expands, love soon follows. Roots reaching toward sunlight find one another underground. The current moves toward the Southeast.

Southeast — The Garden of Blessings (Abundance, Growth, Gratitude)

Here, the wood element matures, branches thicken, and leaves gather light into nourishment. The Southeast is where gratitude becomes tangible, where giving and receiving are no longer opposites.

Reflect:

- **What am I cultivating that feeds more than myself?**
- **Where does generosity come easily and where does it resist flow?**
- **Can abundance be measured not by what I have, but by what circulates?**

To honor this direction is to tend without clutching, to give thanks before the harvest.

Abundance ripens through care, not accumulation. And when growth reaches its fullness, the energy arcs upward again, toward fire, expression, and the clarity of vision.

SOUTH — THE RADIANCE OF BEING SEEN (FAME, ILLUMINATION, PRESENCE)

The South blazes with the element of fire. It is the place of visibility, of purpose revealed. Here we do not seek the light. We become it.

Reflect:

- **What truth longs to be expressed through me?**
- **Where do I hide from my own brilliance?**
- **Can I let illumination be shared, not possessed?**

Fire teaches that to shine is to offer warmth, not burn. Visibility is not vanity, but transparency, letting the inner flame meet the outer world. When the fire's work is done, it softens into embers, with warmth returning to intimacy, light to devotion. The path curves toward the Southwest.

SOUTHWEST — THE HEARTH OF CONNECTION (RELATIONSHIPS, LOVE, SUPPORT)

After the blaze comes glow, the warmth that sustains. The Southwest holds the energy of earth and partnership. It's the ground where love grows slowly, with patience and presence.

Reflect:

- **What relationships in my life bring me home to myself?**
- **Where can I soften my expectations into empathy?**
- **How can I offer steadiness instead of striving?**

Love, like fertile soil, deepens through tending. It is the practice of reciprocity made visible, giving roots to joy and refuge to sorrow. And from this ground of companionship, reflection turns inward again, toward identity, truth, and the courage to stand as oneself.

WEST — THE HARVEST OF THE SELF (COMPLETION, CREATIVITY, CHILDREN)

The West is the season of ripening, where what has been created comes into form. It is the moment before release, when fruit swells with the memory of the sun.

Reflect:

- **What am I ready to finish, to release, or to celebrate?**
- **What creation bears my signature but no longer needs my control?**
- **How do I honor endings as beginnings in disguise?**

This is the domain of creativity, of the deep exhale. In letting go, we make room for wonder. And as light fades, discernment awakens, The gaze that knows what to keep and what to yield. The energy curves northwest, where experience transforms to insight once more.

NORTHWEST — THE RETURNING WIND (MENTORSHIP, GUIDANCE, LEGACY)

Here, air cools and clears. The Northwest is the elder's direction, where wisdom gathered through living becomes a gift to others.

Reflect:

- **What guidance moves through me that was once given to me?**
- **How can I speak less to instruct and more to invite?**
- **What legacy is not built but breathed with the subtle influence of example?**

Wind teaches us that influence travels unseen. The breath we release becomes the air another inhales. So too with wisdom. What we share continues beyond us, moving through generations of wings and words. And so, the circle closes, returning to still water, to purpose renewed, to the quiet pulse of life breathing through all.

CENTER — THE BREATHING EARTH (BALANCE, PRESENCE, BELONGING)

At the center is no direction, only the place where all directions meet. This is the heart of the home, the still point of the turning world. Here, we return to the Tai Chi, the Earth itself, where balance is not perfection, but participation.

Reflect:

- **What grounds me when I lose my way?**
- **How can I listen to the rhythm of enough?**
- **Can I let belonging be simple? Just breath, gravity, and gratitude?**

The Center is not an arrival. It is a remembering. The bagua breathes again.

Closing Note: When the Bagua Lives Again

When you finish the reflections, you may notice your home feels different. Not because the furniture arrangement has changed, but because you have. The act of attending rearranges the space as surely as moving a chair or opening a window.

Feng Shui, at its heart, was never about a perfect arrangement. It is a dialogue between wind and wall, between body and earth, between the seen and unseen. The circle of the Bagua is alive because you are. It moves as you move, rests when you rest.

The ancients read the land by touch and scent, by shadow and sound. You are doing the same when you pause long enough to feel the quiet shift of balance in your own home, in your own breath, in every aspect of your being.

There will be days when the flow feels effortless. Light falling in just the right place, a bird crossing your line of sight at the perfect moment. And there will be days of clutter and dissonance, when the current tangles and you lose your way. Both belong. Both are part of the rhythm.

To live with the world is to let the circle keep turning, giving and receiving, expanding and returning, again and again.

So let the air move through you. Let the seasons rearrange you. And when the world feels out of balance, remember: balance is never stillness. It is always the breath between things.

PART THREE
THE HOUSE THAT BREATHES

Before a home is a structure, it is a meeting place of forces.

Light gathers. Air drifts. Heat pools in certain corners and slips away from others. Even when we sleep, the house continues its quiet exchanges, exhaling warmth into the night, absorbing the scent of rain, releasing the day's accumulated breath.

We often imagine our dwellings as containers, something set apart from weather and season. But if you stand for a moment at the threshold of any doorway, just there where the inner air meets the outer, you can feel how porous a home truly is. The wind carries a hint of cut grass or pavement. The warmth from inside climbs to meet it. Something subtle circulates between the two, a mingling rather than a division.

Birds understand this intuitively. Their nests are never sealed shut; they are woven to breathe. Every twig and strand is placed not to barricade the world out but to make a small pocket where life can be held safely in conversation with its surroundings. A good nest doesn't isolate. It harmonizes. Our homes can do the same.

This part of the book is an invitation to notice the living patterns within the places we inhabit. To sense how light shapes mood, how airflow affects thought, how materials carry the memory of forests, clay, and fields. Not as a critique, not as a call to perfection, but as a gentle widening of perception. When we recognize a home as an ecology rather than an object, we begin to understand that its well-being and ours are braided.

To tend a home is to participate in weaving back our connection to life itself, not by judging what should be different, but by listening for what wants to breathe more freely.

In the chapters ahead, we'll explore how modern culture reduced Feng Shui into something decorative and easily sold, and how we might return to something quieter and more relational. We will reimagine luck as alignment with the forces that already support life, and we will remember how the body itself responds to the shape of a room the same way a bird responds to the lift of wind.

This is not about getting everything "right." It is about letting the home remember its place in the larger circulation of the world and letting ourselves remember that too.

CHAPTER THIRTEEN

THE HOME AS A LIVING ECOSYSTEM

The doorway is always where the exchange begins.

Most mornings on the high plains, before my day takes its shape, I pause at the sliding glass door to the backyard. I don't step through it. I simply hover there in that slim seam where two climates meet. Cool wind moves toward me, carrying the faint dryness of last year's grasses. Behind me, the warmth gathered by the windows drifts forward as if to greet it. For a brief moment, the air folds into itself, inside meeting outside, warmth meeting chill, breath meeting breath.

It's in that narrow place that it becomes clear that my home isn't separate from the land around it. It is a human structure, replying to the living terrain's cues and contours. The walls don't end the conversation. They simply rephrase it.

Inside, the living room plants lean toward the growing light of morning. The monstera spreads another exuberant leaf, a green that feels like muscle and memory. The old Christmas cactus, an heirloom of people I've loved and lost, blooms deep red and white on its own rhythm, taking note of the changing season. These plants, some nearly as old as whole chapters of my life, are not decoration. They are other forms of participation. They metabolize light and memory. Their presence reminds me that the house is not an object containing life. It is a habitat hosting it.

Biophilic design is the modern word for what is actually an ancient truth. We function best not in isolation from nature, but in contact with it. The body softens when surrounded by other living forms because we evolved inside a conversation that never excluded us. Feng Shui, at its root, is not a technique for arranging interiors but an invitation to recognize that the interior world is already porous, already in dialogue with wind and water.

Qi doesn't pause at the threshold. It travels through light. It travels through living beings. It travels wherever attention flows.

When the southeast sun angles into the room in winter, even though the house itself faces northwest, the space warms like a sheltered eddy behind a river stone. The plants transform that warmth into oxygen, moisture, and color. What looks like stillness is actually circulation, exchange, an elegant choreography of breath.

A house is an ecosystem.

And yet not every space in a home is equally alive. A seldom-used guest room may accumulate a kind of quiet that isn't restful but unmoving. Feng Shui does not call this "bad," only uninhabited, the way an untouched corner of meadow grows still when no animal steps through it. Stagnation is not a moral failure; it's an ecological signal.

Something needs presence. Something needs movement. Something needs to be witnessed. Life requires participants.

So, I return often to the thresholds, the literal ones and the more subtle ones. The place where indoor air meets outdoor wind. The spot where light bends around a corner. The spot where warmth pools on a rug or a plant tilts towards its unseen benefactor. These are the openings where a home remembers it is not apart, but a part.

What if welcoming the world in, even a crack of a window, even a moment of noticing, is the authentic Feng Shui?

The land does not end at the property line. The river of Qi does not halt at the sill of a window. The home breathes because the Earth breathes through it. And when we honor that, even a small, ordinary house becomes a living cell in the body of the world.

PRACTICES FOR THE HOME AS A LIVING ECOSYSTEM

Practice 1: Threshold Blessing

Where two worlds meet, pause.

Choose a doorway, either interior or exterior. Stand in the threshold and let yourself be still for a moment longer than feels necessary.

Notice with your senses: The way the air shifts from one side to the other. The faint difference in temperature on your skin. The way light changes color as it crosses materials. The slight change in sound, muted inside, open, or echoing outside. The soft tug of movement, as if the space is breathing around you.

Then slowly let your attention widen until you feel yourself *included* in this exchange, not the observer of it, but a participant in an ancient passage.

When you're ready, offer a blessing that rises from that place of belonging:

As I cross this threshold, may I be met with clarity and kindness. May what is behind me rest. May what is ahead of me open. May this home and this body know each other well.

And then, as you move through into a new space:

"Thank you for receiving me."

When you leave again, pause just a moment in the departing light: "Thank you for letting me go."

Thresholds are the lungs of a home. What you notice becomes breath. What you bless becomes passage.

PRACTICE 2: THE LISTENING WINDOW

Choose a single window, one that feels neutral, ordinary, or overlooked.

Each morning, even for a few seconds, open it. Let the day's first breath find you. Attend to the subtleties: The scent of the air, whether dry, sweet, mineral, or damp. The texture of the wind on your cheek. The temperature resting on your hands. The earliest sounds: a bird call, a distant hum, a hush. How the world announces itself without hurry.

Let this window become a tiny observatory of change. Notice how no two mornings repeat themselves, the way Qi arrives in a new dialect each day. You are not just listening *outward*. You are letting the land remind you what part of you is waking.

Close the window slowly, as if sealing a letter of gratitude.

Carry that small exchange into the rest of your morning.

PRACTICE 3: LIGHT AND SHADOW HOUR

Choose dawn or dusk, the two hours when the home reveals its secret movements. Turn off artificial lights if possible. Sit somewhere simple: a floor cushion, a corner chair, the edge of a bed.

Observe how the room shifts itself: How shadows lengthen and soften. How light climbs a wall or spills across a floor. How color warms or cools. How the energy of the space quiets or brightens. How your own body responds. Does it settle, reach, soften, listen?

Let yourself be a witness to the home practicing Yin and Yang.

The space is not static. It is performing its subtle choreography, adjusting itself as the Earth turns. This is not meditation in the strict sense. It is an apprenticeship; learning how your home speaks its natural language of light.

Stay for a few breaths longer than convenient. Stay until you feel the room's temperament shift and your body shift with it.

Leave the moment gently, as if not to disturb a sleeping animal.

CHAPTER FOURTEEN
WHEN FENG SHUI WAS TAMED

Somewhere in the course of Feng Shui's long journey, a gentle narrowing occurred, not out of malice, but out of human habit. We have a way of taking living things and simplifying them so they are easier to carry. A practice once rooted in wind, water, and careful listening drifted toward diagrams, objects, and quick solutions. What began as a way of reading the land slowly became something that could be bought, taught in a weekend, condensed to a list of dos and don'ts.

It wasn't wrong. It was human.

In many places, Feng Shui became a décor language of mirrors, crystals, and lucky colors. A way to coax "good fortune" or soften the edges of modern life. These gestures aren't meaningless. Many hold real beauty. But when the practice is lifted too far from its origins, something subtle can slip away. We lose the conversation.

Birds never confuse nesting with ownership. They don't upgrade their nests for status. They build for shelter, safety, warmth, guided by wind angles, predators' sightlines, and the shape of branches. Their architecture is responsive, not prescriptive. What looks instinctual is actually exquisite perception.

Early Feng Shui was like that, a relational attunement. A method of asking *How is the land moving today? Where does water pause? Where does wind gather?*

What does this place need from me?

When Feng Shui became commodified, the questions didn't disappear. They became quieter. Beneath every modern tip of where to place a mirror or avoid clutter lies an older inquiry about flow, reciprocity, and relationship.

This isn't about correcting what Feng Shui became. It's about remembering and including what it has always known. We can hold the old and the new at once, honoring the accessible forms without losing touch with the deeper current. When we return to the elemental wisdom beneath the methods, Feng Shui becomes less about fixing a home and more about entering into a relationship with it.

A practice that was mislaid can be coaxed open to memory again.

It can breathe.

CHAPTER FIFTEEN

REIMAGINING LUCK AS ALIGNMENT

Luck is often spoken of as something that arrives from outside. A blessing, a coincidence, a streak of fortune drifting toward us. But in many traditional cosmologies, luck wasn't something to attract. It was something to align with. A kind of ease that appears when actions, intentions, and surroundings move in the same direction.

In the natural world, alignment is everywhere.

A flock turns as one body, not because each bird is lucky, but because each bird is listening. A seed germinates when warmth, moisture, and season coincide. A hawk finds lift, not through force, but by moving in quiet response to the subtle shifts of invisible thermals rising from the land.

None of these outcomes are accidents. None are achievements. They are meetings.

When Feng Shui is understood relationally, luck becomes less about acquiring advantage and more about participating in coherence. It is not something added to a life, but something that arises from how a life is lived. Luck emerges when our choices move in rhythm with the conditions that support them. It comes when timing is respected, when effort meets the right moment, when the home, the body, and the wider world are not working at cross-purposes.

When we honor the contour of the season rather than pushing against it, attend to the health of the ecosystem that sustains us, and care for the well-being of the home that shelters us, friction lessens. Decisions require less force. Opportunities feel less strained. What we often call "good luck" is simply the experience of being carried forward by systems we are no longer resisting.

Luck is the felt sense of belonging. It might show itself as a clarity that wasn't there before, a room that feels easier to breathe in, a conversation that softens, the return of motivation where stagnation once sat, or simply the gentle ease that comes when life stops pushing against itself.

Ecological abundance tends to occur where relationships are healthy. When water moves freely, riparian zones flourish. When a forest recovers from disturbance, new growth invites new life. When a home is tended with attention, warmth and well-being accumulate. Not as excess, but as sufficiency felt in the body.

A space that offers comfort, beauty, and ease quiets the restless hunger for more. When we feel sheltered, nourished, and at home, we are less compelled to consume for reassurance. Energy once spent chasing satisfaction becomes available for discernment, care, and stewardship. From this steadiness, emotional, material, and even financial resources are more likely to gather and endure. Abundance, then, is not a windfall, but a condition created when contentment makes wiser use of what already flows toward us.

Luck, in this way, is not a reward. It is a communion. It arises when we are in right relation with place, timing, responsibility, climate, and our own interior weather.

To reimagine luck as alignment is to let go of the idea that fortune must be summoned or deserved. It is not a desperate calling for outer miracles. Instead, we practice noticing the currents already moving around us, and adjusting gently so our lives move with them rather than against them.

Luck is the feeling of life saying yes. Not because we asked for more, but because we listened more closely.

PRACTICE: FEEDING THE HOUSE, ALIGNING WITH LUCK

Luck is what emerges when a relationship is tended. To "feed" the house is not to charm fortune toward you. It is to participate in the coherence that makes ease possible.

Each day, offer your home one small act of nourishment. Let it be simple, ordinary, almost humble:

- placing a vase of branches where light can touch them
- watering a plant that has been quietly waiting
- opening curtains so the day can enter
- sweeping the floor to let movement return
- lighting a candle at dusk to mark the turning of time
- setting out a bowl of fruit as a gesture of abundance
- playing music that brings life and softness to the space

Do this not as a task, but as a meeting. As you offer the gesture, pause long enough to notice what shifts. Does the room feel clearer? Does your breath deepen? Does something in you settle, or brighten, or open?

This is alignment; the moment when your action, your intention, and the room's response move in the same direction.

Feeding the house is how luck begins to gather. Not as magic, not as reward, but as reciprocity: a quiet yes arising where relationship is healthy.

Offer one gift a day. Receive the ease that returns.

CHAPTER SIXTEEN

CARING FOR THE HOME AS AN ACT OF RECIPROCITY

House cleaning is not usually framed as a sacred act. But it can be.

To tidy, to organize, to sweep, to mend. These gestures can feel like burdens in a culture that values efficiency and productivity. Housework is often treated as a nuisance, a thief of leisure, a cycle with no satisfying conclusion. The counter is clean until the next spill. The floor is spotless until paws or shoes track in the world again. Laundry is neatly folded only until something is worn. The bed is made only to be undone at night.

Domestic life is not a one-and-done affair. It is cyclical, rhythmic, and relational.

And because it is ongoing, many people feel irritation or resignation. *Again?* we mutter, staring at a sink of dishes. *Already?* we think as we sweep up crumbs that seem to multiply. But beneath the repetition is a quiet truth. The home is alive in its own way, and a relationship with anything alive requires ongoing attention.

We understand this in our human bonds.

Imagine saying "I love you" to a partner once and expecting that single declaration to sustain the relationship forever. Imagine cooking one meal, offering one kindness, giving one gesture of care, and believing the work is done. Relationships thrive because they are tended again and again, not out of obligation, but out of affection and recognition.

Homes are no different. A house that shelters our dreams, supports our rest, and holds our sorrows deserves to be met with presence in return.

To maintain a home is to participate in reciprocity at the scale of domestic life. Every act of care becomes a small conversation. The home supports us, and we support the home. The exchange is continuous, as are all living exchanges.

Cleaning, in this light, becomes less about perfection and more about participation. When we sweep a floor, we create openings for Qi to move again. When we wipe a surface, we let light reach places that have been waiting. When we repair a hinge or stitch a tear, we relieve the house of a little of its accumulated weight.

In return, the home steadies us. Rooms seem brighter. Corners feel less heavy. The air tastes different.

Attention is a form of devotion.

Nothing in nature remains vibrant without touch. A forest untended collects fallen branches; a corner of the house no one visits accumulates dust. Neither is shameful. Both are invitations to return to relationship.

And in that return, we are reminded of abundance.

The oven that needs cleaning again means we had food to cook. The laundry piling up means we have clothes to wear. The floors collecting crumbs mean there was a meal shared, or children playing, or the dog returning with news of the yard. Dust on the furniture means we have furniture to support our comfort, shelter, and warmth.

Sometimes what feels like a complaint is really a sign of how fortunate we are.

Every home contains a story of abundance if we look closely. A stocked pantry. Running water that arrives and departs without fanfare. A roof that holds back rain and snow. A space to sleep safely. Light that moves across a room.

Gratitude softens the edges of repetition. It doesn't erase the work but gives it meaning.

Feng Shui, in its most intimate expression, understands that life flows where relationship is tended. When we employ Feng Shui to support our goals and dreams, we are entering into a partnership with the space itself. But a partnership cannot be one-sided. If we ask our home to hold us, we must hold it in return.

This does not require rigid routines or perfect order. It asks only for presence. A wipe of the table can be an acknowledgment. A made bed can be a gesture of steadiness. A freshly opened window can be an invitation to breathe. Letting go of an object can be a small liberation for the space and for ourselves.

Homes respond to care just as people do. To tend a house is not to impose order but to maintain conversation. It is a living reciprocity, a rhythm of mutual maintenance.

When we treat the home as a companion rather than a possession, as a being that absorbs, responds, shelters, and listens, something shifts. The work becomes less a burden and more an act of connection. Caring for the home becomes a way of caring for ourselves, for the life that passes through us, and for the quiet ecology in which we are embedded.

In tending the home gently, repeatedly, we practice a truth the natural world has known forever. Relationship is sustained through ongoing care. Not once, but over and over again. Not perfectly, but faithfully. Not as obligation, but as connection.

PRACTICE: A PRACTICE OF RETURNING

Choose one small task to do today. Find a corner to dust, a window to open, or a sink to clear.

Before you begin, pause. Notice your breath. Notice the room. Feel how the home has been holding you.

Then tend the task slowly, without rushing to the next. Let presence be more important than efficiency.

When you finish, place a hand on your heart or the newly tended space and gently ask: What in my life also needs a simple return? Where have I withdrawn attention from a relationship that still wants tending?

Let the answer arise without judgment.

Because the home teaches what all living relationships teach. Care is not measured by perfection, but by return.

CHAPTER SEVENTEEN

THE BODY'S FENG SHUI

Awe often arrives before understanding, not as an idea, but as a sensation.

For me, it begins in the chest, a soft widening beneath the sternum, as if a small aperture opens. Warmth gathers there, spreading gently inward and outward at once. The mind quiets not because I tell it to, but because the body momentarily remembers its place in a larger pattern.

Awe is the body re-entering relationship.

This is the foundation of Feng Shui inside us. Not correctness. Not belief. Not technique. But experiencing the way the breath shifts when you step beneath tall cottonwoods, or how your pulse slows when rain begins to fall, or how a room can feel immediately welcoming or subtly uneasy before a single thought has formed.

We are not separate from wind and water, movement and stillness; we are composed of them. The minerals that form the bones of the mountains also form our own. The same flow that moves through creeks moves through our veins.

What the ancients described as Qi was never a metaphor. It was an attempt to name the living exchange between inner and outer worlds, the continual movement through which life maintains itself.

Science may describe these exchanges differently, as ions, hormones, or neuroception, but the lived experience remains the same. The body responds to the shape of the world in real time.

When you feel peace in a meadow, something in you is aligning with the openness around you. When a certain room makes your shoulders tighten, your body is registering stagnation long before your mind interprets it. When the smell of soil after rain lifts your spirit, it is the membrane of your awareness becoming momentarily more permeable.

Qi is how the body listens. Feng Shui, at its root, asks us to honor this listening. Not by analyzing every sensation, but by trusting that perception is relational. The body responds because something in the world is speaking, and something in us is speaking back.

In this sense, the body is not a private interior. It is a threshold.

Just as a home breathes with the land around it, the body breathes with the places it inhabits. Every inhalation carries the particulate signature of a moment: light, pollen, humidity, temperature, memory. Every exhalation becomes food for leaves, warmth for air currents, a small contribution to the ongoing conversation.

The body practices Feng Shui when the breath deepens in a quiet room, the skin prickles as a storm approaches, the chest loosens when clutter is cleared, the shoulders drop in soft evening light, or the heart steadies at the sound of birds. These are not arbitrary responses. They are signals of a living being navigating the currents around itself.

If a home becomes stagnant, the body often feels it first. If a landscape is thriving, the body senses that too, through ease, clarity, or the faint unwinding of tension. Our physiology is porous, tuned to changes in airflow, temperature, pattern, and emotional tone.

Awe, then, is not an isolated feeling. It is a doorway. It suspends our usual ways of knowing just enough for perception to widen again. In awe, the boundaries become permeable, and the world enters us more freely. We meet it not as observers but as participants, membranes exchanging meaning.

Understanding this doesn't require us to interpret every sensation or to assign moral weight to our responses. Instead, it invites a gentler relationship with the body's signals, an openness to the possibility that the body is always in conversation with place.

To tend the body's Feng Shui is to pay attention to what enlivens and what dims. Where breath deepens and where it catches. Where stillness restores and where motion clarifies.Where the body feels welcomed, and where it waits at the edges.

The world does not ask us to master these sensations. It asks us only to notice them. Because noticing is how we find our way back into alignment: not with a system of rules, but with the living rhythm that threads through air, soil, water, home, and the body itself.

A bird calls outside the window. Somewhere beneath your feet, the soil breathes.

And here, within, the quiet shifts as inner and outer rhythms meet again.

PRACTICE 1: THE THREE-BREATH RESET

Wherever you find yourself, whether in a kitchen, office, doorway, or meadow, pause as if you are stepping into a small clearing.

Breath 1: Arrive

Let the first inhale simply *place you* in the moment. Feel your feet meet the ground, your weight settling, the temperature of the air touching your skin.

Notice the space around you as if it is noticing you in return.

Breath 2: Soften

With the second breath, release whatever the body is holding: the jaw, the shoulders, the micro-tensions. Softening isn't collapse. It's permission. It lets Qi begin to circulate again, like a window cracked open.

Breath 3: Listen

With the third breath, widen your awareness. Sense the field around you, the subtle movements of air, the emotional tone of the room, the faint hum of life outside. Let the breath be a membrane, exchanging inside and outside with each cycle.

These three breaths re-establish the relationship, the smallest possible act of Feng Shui inside the body.

PRACTICE 2: FOLLOW ONE SENSATION

Choose a single sensation to anchor your attention: **the weight of your feet on the floor, the gentle rise of your spine, the coolness or warmth of air entering your nostrils, or even the sense of your hands resting where they are.**

Let this one sensation be your doorway. Stay with it for a full minute, long enough for the mind to quiet and the body to reveal more.

Notice how the sensation changes with time. Does it deepen? Warm? Cool? Spread? Soften? Does your awareness grow quieter or more spacious as you stay? This is how perception becomes ecological again, not focused inward *or* outward, but resting in the meeting place between the two.

One sensation, well attended, reconnects you to the present field of Qi.

PRACTICE 3: THE BODY COMPASS

Stand comfortably, with your knees soft and your breath natural. Feel the space around you as if it were a landscape.

Gently ask yourself: **"Where is ease?"** Not as a mental question, but a bodily one.

Then turn slowly. A quarter turn, half turn, full circle, until some part of you brightens: the breath deepens, the chest loosens, the skin tingles, your posture subtly lifts, or you feel a faint sense of "yes" without reason.

This is your directional Qi for the moment, the orientation where your body feels most aligned with the environment. You don't need to understand it or justify it. The body does not speak in reasons. It speaks in sensations, in ease and resistance, in subtle yeses and quiet noes.

Just let it guide one small choice today. Which way you face during a break, where you sit for a moment of rest, which path you take on a walk, or simply which direction you breathe toward.

The body knows how to navigate the world's currents because it is part of them. All it needs is enough quiet for sensation to rise into its awareness.

PART FOUR
KINSHIP BEYOND THE DOOR

Every home opens outward.

Even the most sheltered room, the most carefully tended corner, is shaped by something larger. By the pattern of rains, by the way wind carries seeds over the roof, or by the quiet migrations of creatures passing through unseen corridors of night. To care for the spaces that we inhabit is to participate in a much wider field of relationships.

Inside, the home breathes with our daily rhythms. Outside, the land breathes with eons of memories. And yet the boundary between them is far more fluid than it appears.

Step past your doorway, and the conversation widens. The same currents of Qi that move through walls and windows also travel through the folds of hills, the bends of rivers, the shifting paths of birds overhead. The world is speaking in many directions at once, and we are invited into that chorus. Not as guests, but as kin.

Birds have always led the way in this regard. They read weather with their bodies. They sense changes in climate long before we do. They navigate by stars, magnetic fields, coastline, and memory.

Where we build routines, birds build relationships.

The next part of the book turns us toward the world beyond the house, toward the fields, forests, shorelines, and cities we share. It asks how birds can teach us to move through these landscapes with greater awareness, how places carry memory, and how every act of care, from sweeping a doorstep to restoring a watershed, is part of the same quiet ethic of reciprocity.

If Part Three taught us that the home breathes with the world, Part Four reminds us that the world breathes through us as well. This is where Feng Shui widens beyond the walls, not as a philosophy of interiors, but as a way of belonging to Earth.

CHAPTER EIGHTEEN

WHERE THE BIRDS LEAD US

Before I learned to read landscapes, the birds were already doing it.

They move through the world with an attentiveness that is both instinct and intelligence; listening not just with ears, but with feathers, bones, and skin. A shift in wind speed, a subtle drop in pressure, the faint metallic scent that arrives before rain. These are not background details to a bird. They are coordinates.

To follow birds across a landscape is to glimpse how alive the world is beyond our usual thresholds of attention.

A meadow is never just open space. It is a matrix of thermals, seedheads, insects, sheltering shadows, and subtle grades of moisture. A forest is not a collection of trunks but a layered architecture of sound and refuge, each branch a waypoint in a moving map. Even a city, with its cables, vents, scaffolds, and courtyards, becomes a navigable terrain of microclimates and opportunities.

Birds read all of this with a fluency we're only beginning to remember.

When a flock banks in unison into the wind at the same moment, it isn't choreography. It's cohesion. When a single warbler pauses its migration for a day, it may be responding to the faintest atmospheric hint of an approaching storm. When a raven lifts from a rut in the road just before a car arrives, it is not luck but a lived pattern.

Their lives depend on attunement. Ours do as well.

Long before instruments and forecasts, humans watched bird behavior to understand what the weather had in store. The sudden silence of songbirds signaled the presence of a predator. A pre-dawn chorus foretold clear skies. Swallows flying low meant rain. These were not superstitions but observations, relational knowledge woven from generations of listening.

Now, as the climate shifts, birds sense the changes long before we can name them. Migration routes loosen and drift. Arrival times slip out of sync with flowering and hatch cycles. Some species adjust by nesting earlier, moving higher, or learning to use altered habitats. Others cannot. Environmental disruption first manifests in the confused paths of creatures whose survival depends on finely tuned correspondence with the seasons and place.

To watch birds today is to witness both resilience and its limits. There comes a point at which responsiveness is no longer enough, when the pace or scale of change outruns even the most finely tuned lives.

And still, the birds persist.

They experiment. They reroute. They adapt where adaptation is possible. They reveal that resilience is not rigidity, but responsiveness, the ability to notice change early, to adjust without panic, to conserve energy by moving with conditions rather than against them.

Even in altered landscapes, birds continue to teach.

A bird practices Feng Shui without abstraction. It reads the direction of shelter. It senses the flow of air through a stand of trees. It chooses a nesting site where life can circulate freely. It moves, again and again, according to what the world offers now, not what it once offered.

This is not mystical. It is relational literacy.

As humans, we do not need to mimic avian precision, but we can learn from their way of being. We can develop the capacity to pause when the wind shifts, to notice what changes in light and sound, to feel the body respond before the mind rushes to interpret. Birds remind us that resilience begins with perception, that responding well depends on noticing early.

They invite us back into the larger pattern not to master it, but to trust that belonging is cultivated through attention. When we begin to follow their cues, even briefly, the land becomes articulate again. We start to sense the quiet invitations the world offers: a pocket of warm air, a sheltered bend in the trail, the hush that gathers before a storm, the sudden brightness after.

These are the coordinates of relationship. Birds trace them every day. And if we let them, they can lead us back into a way of perceiving that feels not new, but ancestral.

A way of being that says "You are part of this, too."

REFLECTION: THE FIRST GESTURE OF BELONGING

Pause at the threshold where inside becomes outside. Let the moment be unrushed. Birds never rush into a space. They read it first. The pressure, the light, the movement of air.

Stand there long enough to notice what is changing.

The ground holds your weight. A current of wind brushes your cheek. The temperature is slightly different from what it was a moment ago. Somewhere nearby, a bird adjusts its call because you have entered its field.

You are not intruding. You are entering a relationship with your surroundings.

Let this awareness settle in the chest, and find that familiar soft widening that comes when something in you remembers the world is alive and responsive. Then notice what the body asks for next.

A shift of stance. A deeper breath. A step into shade or sun. A pause instead of forward motion.

Respond gently, the way a bird does. Not by forcing certainty, but by adjusting to what is present.

Offer the simplest gesture of belonging: "I see you." Not as a claim, but as participation.

In responding to what you feel, even if the adjustment is minor, you practice resilience. You rehearse the art of staying in relationship as conditions change.

CHAPTER NINETEEN

THE SPIRIT OF PLACE

The first place I ever listened to was a creek that cut through the edge of suburbia. It was a narrow ribbon of water threading between cottonwoods and the cracked backs of sunbaked fields. As a child, I followed it as though it were a teacher. I knew where the shallow pools gathered after rain, where the minnows flashed silver in sunlight, where the frogs hid in their green silence.

Sometimes, when the water ran low, I'd kneel to watch the tadpoles wriggling in the warm shallows, their bodies glistening like drops of moving ink. I cupped them in my palms, a small universe shifting between my fingers. I didn't yet know the word *metamorphosis*, but I felt the truth of it, that change was the most natural language the earth spoke.

That creek was my first classroom in Feng Shui, long before I ever knew its concepts. It showed me that water listens to the land. It bends, gathers, waits, and moves according to contour and invitation. Each turn of the stream, each bend around stone, was a gesture of relationship.

As I grew older, the landscape widened. The creek's whisper gave way to the wind that swept the high plains and the thunder that rolled down from the mountains. I learned the shape of awe when standing among ponderosa and aspen at altitude, breath thinning, sky pressing close enough to feel its pulse in my ribs.

The mountains carried a different kind of intelligence. Vast, patient, unhurried. Their stillness wasn't absence of motion but the presence of time, deep time, the kind that shapes without haste. Among their slopes, I began to understand that every place has a voice, but you have to match its tempo to hear it.

In classical Chinese thought, this presence is often described through **Shen,** the spirit or vitality that animates all living things, from humans to deities to mountains and rivers. Shen is not a ghostly essence. It is the shimmering interior life of a place, the way consciousness expresses itself through relationship.

And when Shen is expressed through the land itself, ancient texts call it **Di Shen,** the spirit of nature, the presence that arises wherever earth, water, wind, fire, and time gather in conversation. Di Shen is the character of a creek at dusk, the mood of a high plain under starlight, the intelligence of a gull riding thermals above a harbor. It is the land's way of being awake.

Every place carries this presence: an emotional, ecological, and historical texture that is difficult to define but unmistakable when felt. Some landscapes greet you with spaciousness, others with a subtle alertness. Some feel woven with memory. Some feel shy. Some feel wounded.

When you arrive somewhere new, your body often knows its Di Shen before your thoughts catch up. The shoulders tilt back slightly. The breath deepens or holds. The senses widen. The nervous system adjusts its listening.

This is Qi interacting with Qi. Consciousness meeting consciousness. Your Shen brushing against the Di Shen of the land.

When this kind of listening is practiced over time, it becomes more than a momentary impression. It becomes rootedness. The place stops feeling like a backdrop you pass through and becomes something you belong to and are responsible for. Rootedness changes the quality of attention. It turns observation into relationship, and relationship into care.

A place is shaped by geology, by water, by past fires or floods, by the migrations of animals, by the footprints of ancestors, by the patterns of wind. But it is also shaped by what we bring to it: our noticing, our behavior, our griefs and blessings. A place responds. When we treat land as inert, it retreats into quiet. When we treat it with curiosity, something opens.

Over time, that opening works on us as well. To know a place intimately is to be less helpless within it. Familiarity replaces abstraction. Patterns become legible. Issues that once felt overwhelming begin to feel actionable, not because the challenges are smaller, but because we are no longer strangers to them.

To enter a place well is to arrive slowly, without assumptions. To pause before stepping deeper. To let the land introduce itself.

Sometimes, I stand at the edge of a field and wait. I listen to the timbre of the wind, the posture of the grasses, the mood of the birds. There is no analysis in this, only presence. Eventually, the field feels less like an object to walk through and more like a being to walk with.

Places hold memory, too. A town built along a river carries the river's patience and volatility. A desert plateau holds the clarity of open sky. A post-industrial district remembers extraction. A prairie remembers fire, grazing, and long horizons.

When we allow ourselves to be shaped by this memory, when we stay long enough to learn what a place has endured and what it still needs, we begin to locate ourselves within a larger story. Isolation softens. Community becomes possible. Not just community with other people, but with the more-than-human lives whose futures are braided with our own.

And yet every place also longs for relationship. Not to be fixed or idealized, but to be witnessed, honored, understood.

Feng Shui at the scale of landscape is not about control. It is about reciprocity. It asks: **How can we move in ways that support the spirit of a place rather than diminish it? What does this land need from us to thrive again?**

To ask this question sincerely is to step out of passivity. Advocacy does not begin with expertise. It starts with attachment. We protect what we love, and we love what we know intimately enough to be changed by. Rootedness turns concern into commitment, and commitment into collective care.

To me, the spirit of place is less an external deity and more a kind of memory that lives in wind and soil. The land remembers everything that has ever passed through it: the floods and fires, the migrations, the laughter of children by a creek. When you return to a place that once knew you, it greets you not as a stranger but as someone it has been holding in its archive of wind and soil. Perhaps that's why I still return, in memory and in body, to the high plains and the mountain creeks, because they remind me of my earliest conversation with the world.

Everywhere I've lived since, I've sought that feeling. The way a place, when you really listen, begins to rearrange you. Some spaces sharpen the mind; others slow the heart until you can hear what's beneath it. The spirit of place is not something you summon. It's something that begins to speak once you're quiet enough to listen.

In the end, every place we love asks the same question in its own dialect of wind or water, sunlight or silence: **Will you listen?**

Because listening is how bonds begin.

REFLECTION: LISTENING FOR THE GENIUS OF PLACE

Begin wherever you are. Step outside, or if you cannot, open a window.

Let the air cross the threshold between inside and out, that invisible seam where exchange happens.

Pause. Don't name what you see yet. Just listen.

Every place has its own frequency: the hum of insects, the pulse of wind in branches, the layered rhythm of traffic and birdsong. These are not background noises. They are the voice of the place speaking in its native tongue.

Stay still long enough for perception to widen. Feel how the ground holds you. Notice what draws your attention first. A patch of shifting light, the smell of warm soil, the call of a single bird? That first draw is the land inviting you into dialogue.

Stay with that invitation. The longer you listen, the more specific it becomes. Over days and seasons, listening turns into familiarity. Familiarity turns into responsibility. This is how a place stops feeling distant or overwhelming and starts feeling like something you can stand up for alongside others who love it too.

Ask quietly, in the way a body asks when it listens: **What do you remember that I've forgotten? What do you need from me?**

There may be no answer or only silence. But even silence has texture. It is the pause the land takes before speaking again.

Listening is a kind of offering.

When you attend to a place without demanding meaning, you begin to participate in its aliveness.

From this participation, community naturally grows. You begin to recognize who else is listening. Neighbors, birds, trees, watersheds. Shared care weaves relationships among humans and across species. Protection becomes less about fighting and more about tending. Watching out for one another and for the place that holds you all.

This is the heart of Feng Shui, beneath and beyond walls. Not rearranging matter, but rearranging attention. Not designing for perfection, but dwelling in relationship.

To dwell well is to listen well. To listen well is to remember that every place is already speaking. And that listening is the first, smallest, most powerful act of belonging. From belonging comes responsibility, and from responsibility, the quiet courage to protect what has given you a place to stand.

CHAPTER TWENTY

RECIPROCITY - THE ECOLOGY OF GRACE

When we open the door, things come in: light, air, the scent of rain, the dust of faraway places. But even when the door is closed, the exchange never stops. Every home is porous, breathing through vents, fibers, and cracks. Every act of living draws something in and releases something else.

The air we exhale becomes food for leaves. The warmth from our bodies radiates into the walls. The water that swirls down a drain eventually finds its way to the soil or the sea. Even the objects we bring inside, like the wood of a table or the cotton of a sheet, carry the memory of forests and fields.

Our homes are not endpoints of consumption. They are nodes in a living network of transformation.

We tend to forget this. In modern life, the walls feel solid, the supply lines invisible. We buy, use, and discard, and the movement vanishes from view. But the land does not forget. Energy does not end where our awareness does.

Feng Shui, at its quiet heart, has always been about reciprocity. Wind and water are in continual exchange. Qi is flowing through and between. To live in balance is not to freeze the flow but to recognize its direction, and to give back as much life as we draw in.

In my own home, I try to remember this by paying attention to what moves through the space. The air from the open window. The warmth of the sun that powers the solar panels. The water flowing into and out of the pipes. Each is a guest passing through. Each deserves gratitude.

The same is true of what we let go. Waste is not a disappearance, but a relocation. Compost returns to soil. Heat rises into the atmosphere. Words and emotions we release linger, shaping the tone of the room long after they're spoken. We do not act in isolation.

Reciprocity is not about guilt. It is about relationship, the way a river gives and takes along its course, shaping banks even as it's shaped by them. When we understand ourselves as part of this greater system of life, we begin to design and live differently. We buy less and repair more. We plant what pollinators need rather than what pleases us alone. We arrange a space so air and light can circulate freely, not only for beauty but for vitality.

When gratitude is present, care follows naturally. What we love, we tend. To live with Feng Shui as reciprocity is to let that love take form in practice. Each act of care, from sweeping a floor, tending a plant, or opening the window to the morning breeze, becomes both an offering and a renewal.

Grace, in this sense, is ecological. It's the awareness that we are constantly participating in the giving and receiving that sustains the world.

We often think of care as something we extend outward to people, animals, plants, and the spaces that hold us. But the older ecologies know that care is never one-directional. Every act of tending initiates a loop.

Offer water, and the soil returns softness. Sweep a floor, and the house exhales. Feed a bird, and its presence alters the air around you. Repair a broken gate, and the path becomes passable for others.

Reciprocity is simply the exchange of attention, energy, nourishment, or protection between living beings. It is the ecology beneath all ecologies.

In some cultures, reciprocity is framed as gratitude. In others, as responsibility, In others still, as balance. But beneath all interpretations lies a single understanding. **Life continues because relationships are tended.**

Birds enact reciprocity constantly.

A chickadee warns the whole forest with its alarm calls. Hummingbirds pollinate flowers, which they will never see bloom again. Crows leave small offerings of twigs, shells, and bits of treasure near the homes of humans who feed them, not as payment but as recognition.

The natural world is not transactional. But it is exquisitely responsive.

A river does not ask what it will gain before it flows. A tree does not measure the return before offering shade. A bird does not calculate repayment before singing at dawn.

The living world does not operate on contracts or guarantees. It does not withhold until conditions are met. Its generosity is not naïve, but it is not conditional in the way human systems often are. And yet, nothing goes unanswered.

When soil is nourished, it softens and holds water longer. When pollinators are fed, they multiply life's abundance. When a place is tended, life leans back toward it. Sometimes quietly, sometimes all at once.

Responsiveness is not bargaining. It is a relationship. It is the way living systems adjust, echo, and reply to one another through time. Care alters conditions. Attention shifts outcomes. Harm leaves traces. Healing does too.

The natural world does not say *I will give only if you give first.*

It says instead: "What you do matters." *What you offer changes the field.*

This is not a ledger. It is a conversation.

Humans sometimes forget this. Modern life encourages us to see our homes, our landscapes, even our own bodies as systems to manage or optimize. But when we shift from ownership to kinship, something softens. Care becomes an offering rather than a chore.

Feng Shui, in its most relational form, invites reciprocity at every scale.

Sweep with intention. Repair with tenderness. Arrange with respect for circulation. Open windows not just for fresh air, but so the house can hear the world. Plant something native as a gesture of belonging. Leave water for migrating birds during drought.

Each small act sends a message: *I am here. I am listening. I am part of this.*

Reciprocity doesn't make life perfect. But it does make life coherent. It restores the invisible threads between self and world, reminding us that we are not isolated actors but participants in the long conversation of Earth.

Grace moves along these threads.

When we begin to see that everything passes through us—air, water, warmth, even memory—it becomes harder to believe in separation. The same current that stirs the leaves in the garden stirs the weather over the mountains. What leaves our homes does not vanish; it joins the long conversation of wind and tide.

But lately, the flow has been faltering. Rivers run too warm. Winds carry smoke instead of rain. The balance that once felt self-healing now trembles under our un-listening.

And yet, the teachings of wind and water remain steady, patient, and available.

They remind us that imbalance is not an ending, but a call to remember flow again: to grieve what's been lost, to tend what still breathes, and to live as though our smallest acts still matter.

Because they do.

REFLECTION: THE FLOW THAT PASSES THROUGH

Sit quietly inside your home. Choose one small flow to follow.

It may be water entering from the tap and leaving through the drain.

It may be light crossing the room as the sun rises or falls.

It may be air entering with your inhale and returning changed.

Trace it gently with your awareness. Where did it come from? Where will it go?

Notice what you feel as you follow its journey. Curiosity? Softness? A faint ache? Gratitude? A sense of belonging?

Then ask, very quietly: **What am I giving back in return?**

Reciprocity begins with that awareness. It doesn't demand perfection. Only participation.

To live with grace is to live as if nothing truly belongs to us, but everything passes through us. And when it does, it carries the imprint of how we tended the relationship.

PRACTICE: THE OFFERINGS PATH

Once a week, leave a small offering outdoors. Not to ask for anything, but to acknowledge what you receive.

It might be: a handful of seeds, a bowl of water, compost for soil, a whispered thank-you.

Let it be simple. Let it be sincere. Let it be an expression of gratitude to the place that holds you.

CHAPTER TWENTY-ONE

THE HOME AS A LIVING MEMBER OF THE ECOSYSTEM

By now, the idea may feel less strange: **your home is part of Earth's metabolism.**

Not metaphorically, literally.

It drinks light, exhales heat, channels air, and absorbs moisture. Its materials exchange temperature with the sky. Its plants breathe with the neighborhood trees. Its sounds mingle with the city or the meadow. Its inhabitants, human or not, shape its Qi moment by moment.

The home is not an island. It is a node in a vast and breathing network.

When we understand this, the purpose of Feng Shui shifts. No longer a practice of optimizing interiors, it becomes a way of participating in ecological flow.

A home aligned with its ecosystem welcomes wind without letting it scream through, receives light without becoming scorched, shelters without severing connection, circulates warmth and coolness as a body does, offers refuge and nourishment to non-human kin, and reflects the character of the land it rests on.

And in return, the ecosystem supports the home with water from near and distant watersheds, with food and energy, with shade and soil, with pollinators and birdsong, with seasons that guide interior rhythms, and with weather that shapes architecture over time.

When the home is recognized as a living member of this greater whole, we become stewards of a relationship, not of a structure. And like all relationships, it deepens through attention.

PART FIVE
RESTORING FLOW

Even the most attuned life slips out of rhythm.

Homes accumulate heaviness. Bodies accumulate tension. Climates shift around us in ways we never expected. And the world, loud with urgency, pulls our attention in a thousand directions.

By now, the birds have led us far beyond the walls of the house. They've shown us how attention is a form of participation, how listening is already a kind of offering, how every place carries a pulse, its own breath, its own interiority.

But kinship does not end with recognition. Once we feel the world responding to us, we also begin to feel where it is strained, where the field has thinned or gone quiet, and where the balance that once sustained so many beings now wavers under the weight of our forgetting.

And so, this final part turns toward **repair,** toward the work of restoring flow in a world that is both exquisitely alive and deeply out of balance. Not by returning to some imagined past, but by re-entering the conversation that has always been underway. Wind meeting wing. Water shaping stone. Home answering weather. Body answering home.

Here we ask how to live Feng Shui as an ecological ethic, a way of arranging not only our rooms but our relationships, our communities, our cities, and the expansive field of the living Earth.

CHAPTER TWENTY-TWO

WHEN THE WORLD IS OUT OF BALANCE

Some mornings, the wind feels different.

It carries the scent of smoke from hundreds of miles away, from forests too dry to remember their own green. Rivers pulse thinner. Snowmelt runs too soon. The world is still speaking, but the tone has changed.

Balance, the ancients knew, was never static. It is the motion between the inhale and exhale, the ebb and return. But lately, the inhale has gone on too long. We have taken more than we've returned, and we've spoken louder than we've listened.

When the world tilts this way, the teachings of Feng Shui become less about placement and arrangement of space and more like an ethic of attention, a discipline of staying awake in a time of unraveling. To live by wind and water now means learning how to grieve without paralysis, to act without the illusion of control.

Grief, in its purest form, is a measure of love. It tells us that the bond is still intact, that even as coral bleaches and rivers burn, we have not become numb. To feel the world's imbalance — the thinning rivers, the ragged tree lines, the silence where a dawn chorus used to be — is to still belong to it. And belonging is the beginning of any repair.

There are days I stand outside and can almost hear the tension in the air, the weight of change pressing down, the ache of species vanishing in silence.

One afternoon, when the smoke from distant fires turned the sun a bruised amber, a red-tailed hawk appeared above the house. She circled slowly, rising on an invisible column of warm air. The world below her was out of balance, but her ascent was steady, deliberate. She rode the day's thermals as they were, not as they should have been.

Watching her, I felt the world's stubborn, aching desire to right itself. Even in disruption, there is movement toward balance. It's not a return to what was, but a reaching for what could still be.

Perhaps this is what Feng Shui requires now. Tending the small harmonies when we can, even as larger ones shift beyond our reach. Opening windows for clean air. Letting the house cool at night to honor the dark. Watering the plants that still lean toward the light. Not because any of these acts will save the world, but because they keep us in conversation with it.

The river's overflow, the flood, or the drought are the earth's way of recalibrating, remembering flow. What feels like chaos is sometimes renewal beginning in disguise.

When we think of Feng Shui as an art of flow, imbalance becomes not a failure but a teacher. It reminds us where the current has stalled, where energy needs to move again. Sometimes the blockage is physical: clutter, noise, pollution. Sometimes it is emotional: despair, denial, the refusal to feel. Both require tending.

Healing begins with movement. Not frantic movement, but honest flow. Healing starts with the willingness to let energy and materials circulate again. Water through the soil. Air through the lungs. Kindness through communities.

We cannot restore balance by force. We can only reopen the channels through which balance remembers how to return.

Imbalance is not a flaw. It is a message. A drought is not a judgment. It is a condition. A storm is not a punishment. It is a reorganization. A cluttered corner is not a failure. It is an invitation.

When a room feels heavy, when a schedule feels airless, when a mind feels scattered, the body is responding to a pattern of Qi that has been disrupted, paused, or pooled. Modern life encourages us to override these sensations. To push through. To adapt. To numb. But the natural world never dismisses imbalance. It responds to it.

The forms of imbalance in modern life are many:

- Clutter: not just objects, but the emotional residue they hold.
- Noise: external, internal, cultural.
- Overwhelm: too many inputs, too little digestion.
- Disconnection: from place, season, body, breath.
- Pace: too fast for perception to keep up.

None of these needs blame. All of them need attention.

Think of a river that slows behind debris. The water gathers, darkens, and stills. The solution is rarely to force movement but to clear a path, to remove just one or two branches so flow can find itself again.

Humans work the same way. When we feel out of balance, the impulse to overhaul everything is strong. But what restores us is usually small and precise. A quiet morning. A swept threshold. A warm meal. A step outside to feel the wind.

Balance isn't a state to achieve. It's a relationship to tend. And when we return even slightly to flow, the world responds.

REFLECTION: THE ART OF TENDING

Find one small imbalance in your daily life. View it not as a problem, but as a conversation. A plant drooping for lack of water. A space in your home that feels stagnant.

A relationship needing nurture.

Approach it not as something to fix, but something to listen to. What is it asking for? Space? Attention? Stillness?

Then offer what you can.

Even a small act of care, whether a glass of water poured, a word spoken gently, a window opened to morning air, reenters you into the circulation of life. Balance is not a destination. It is an ongoing tending. When the world is out of balance, tending is the way back into belonging.

When we begin to tend, even gently, something shifts, not only in the world but in us. The small acts become their own form of prayer. Through them, we reenter the choreography of belonging.

Harmony is not found in grand gestures but in the daily attention that keeps energy moving. The air refreshed, the water circulating, the light invited. Each act of care ripples outward, subtle but real, rejoining the larger pattern that sustains everything.

This is how balance returns. Not all at once, but breath by breath, gesture by gesture.

When we learn to restore balance in our own lives, something subtle but profound awakens. : a memory that flow is possible.

The world's immense imbalances can feel unbearably vast, far beyond the reach of a single human hand. Pollution. Climate unraveling. Extinction. And yet each of these crises is, at its heart, a story of flow interrupted. Waters choked. Air thickened. Habitats severed. Relationships frayed.

What we practice at the scale of a room becomes rehearsal for what we can offer at the scale of a river, a coastline, or a community. Clearing a corner of clutter does not repair the atmosphere. But it restores our capacity to sense where energy has pooled and how to gently invite movement again. It teaches us how to notice. And noticing is the beginning of every restoration.

When we open a window to let fresh air in, we remember that air is shared. When we refill a birdbath, we remember that water is kin. When we compost a handful of scraps, we remember that nothing truly disappears. It only becomes something else.

These gestures are not solutions to global imbalance, but they return us to a relationship with the Earth, which is the ground of every meaningful change.

Nature shows us this constantly.

Consider the Pacific brant, a small, dark goose that once traveled reliably from the tundra of Alaska down the long curve of the Pacific coast to wintering grounds in Mexico. For generations, their migration traced the continent's edge like a moving thread of black and white. But as the climate warms and eelgrass, the brant's primary food, now remains abundant in Alaska through winter, many flocks have begun to stay. They linger where their ancestors could not. They adapt, not by abandoning their lineage, but by listening closely to the world as it shifts beneath them.

The brant reminds us that imbalance is not the end of the story. It is a condition to respond to. A conversation to reenter. Their altered migration is neither triumph nor tragedy. It is a testament to responsiveness, to living beings' ability to seek flow even when the old pathways bend or vanish. If a bird can revise a journey it has taken for centuries, perhaps we can revise the ways we move through our own lives, our homes, and our communities.

A person who knows how to listen to a stagnant room becomes a person who can listen to a struggling ecosystem. A person who practices returning flow in their daily life becomes a person capable of helping restore it where the world needs it most. Small acts of tending cultivate the posture of care needed for the larger acts of protecting watersheds, choosing renewable materials, restoring habitats, and supporting policies that keep future generations in mind.

The scale shifts. The practice remains the same.

Each gesture strengthens the muscle of reciprocity; the willingness to stay in relationship with a world that is still speaking, still adapting, still trying to remember balance. When we tend even the most minor imbalances with sincerity, we prepare ourselves to meet the largest ones with courage. This is how personal attention becomes planetary love.

This is how the world begins, little by little, to breathe again.

CHAPTER TWENTY-THREE

ALIGNMENT WITH THE LIVING WORLD

Sustainability is often framed as personal virtue or sacrifice, as if living lightly were a kind of moral performance. Sustainability in the natural world offers a different interpretation. It is alignment.

Every living being dances to the rhythms of nature: the turning seasons, the shifting tides, the cycles of day and night, the long arcs of migration. When beings live within these cycles, they flourish with an ease that looks almost effortless. When they are pushed out of rhythm, whether by climate pressure, habitat disruption, or scarcity, they strain.

Humans feel this also. The body knows when it is living against the grain.

Sustainability, at its heart, is not a moral stance. It is a return to ecological coherence.

No species can thrive in a depleted or damaged home, and humans are no exception. Every breath, every meal, every safe place to sleep depends on natural systems that have been quietly refining themselves for millions of years. Soil filters water. Plants renew the air. Oceans store heat. Communities of living beings strengthen one another's survival.

When those systems falter, life falters. When they are nourished, life responds.

Sustainability asks us to move in ways that support the systems that support us. Not as heroism. Not as deprivation. But as the simple practice of belonging.

It raises questions that are both practical and intimate:

How do I move in ways that nourish the sources of my nourishment?

How do I choose materials, habits, and patterns that allow life to circulate more freely?

How do I live today in a way that doesn't take tomorrow's breath away from any species, including our own?

Sustainability is not just about the environment. It is also about well-being, equity, and continuing the long arc of care that ensures future generations can drink clean water, breathe clean air, and inhabit places where life is still possible. When framed this way, sustainability becomes a universal necessity for survival, not a lifestyle trend. It is simply the way life protects life.

And this protection can begin with the smallest gestures. Opening a window, letting indoor air rejoin the larger atmosphere. Using light during the hours when light is abundant. Choosing objects that endure, not wear out, from materials that return to the world rather than burden it. Composting as a quiet thank-you to soil, a way of completing a cycle that was never meant to end with scraps in a bin. Walking when you can. Fixing what can be repaired. Sharing when you have more than you need. Planting something native and watching who arrives.

One autumn, a small flock of Western Bluebirds discovered the sand cherry in the backyard. Its branches were bent with ripe fruit, and the dusky pink of early frost was settling on the leaves. They gathered in the branches for days, feasting before their migration. But what struck me most was not their presence. It was their restraint. They ate only what they needed. There was no stripping of branches, no frantic competition. After they moved on, the shrub still held fruit for the robins, sparrows, and rabbits.

It was a quiet choreography of enough-ness. The bluebirds didn't hoard. They didn't optimize. An entire community was fed.

Sustainability becomes possible when it stops being a performance and becomes a relationship, an ongoing practice of moving with the world rather than against it. A way of remembering that what we take is not ours to own, only ours to use for a moment before returning to the cycle.

Birds show us this constantly. A nest is rebuilt each year not because last year's was flawed, but because its materials have returned to the soil. Grasses soften. Feathers drift. Twigs break down. Everything circulates.

A nest is not a possession. It is a temporary gesture of belonging. A seasonal "yes" to a particular place.

Not all birds abandon their nests entirely. Some, like raptors, return to the same place year after year, carefully rebuilding and reinforcing their homes. These nests are not abandoned to dissolve into the elements, but rather restored. Each season's occupants add a layer of continuity, a careful tending to what was once created. This is the beauty of reuse, a way of honoring the past while allowing it to grow with the present. In this way, the nest becomes not only a gesture of belonging but a living testament to cycles of renewal.

When we live sustainably, we echo the understanding that our homes and the larger landscapes that hold them depend on us tending the cycles that sustain life. We often forget the collaboration we're engaged in. We forget how connected we are. We forget how connected our homes are, too.

A home is not an inert container. It is an ecosystem within an ecosystem. It is a microclimate shaped by the interplay of sunlight, humidity, materials, airflow, and the daily weather of human emotion. Wood absorbs moisture. Clay holds coolness. Plants breathe. Shadows migrate. Every object participates in the discourse.

Homes need circulation and renewal as much as birds' nests do. The minutest shifts, such as turning a chair toward morning sun, bringing in a sprig of pine after a walk, or choosing wood or fibers that breathe, ripple through the home's ecology. And because we are porous, they ripple through us too. When we recognize home as a living participant in a greater cycle, we become stewards not of a structure, but of a living bond.

With each sustainable choice, small or large, we align more closely with the living systems that make our lives possible. And in this alignment, something subtle shifts. Life becomes less resistant. Decisions feel clearer. Ease, flow, and even what some traditions call "luck" gather, not as rewards, but as natural consequences of moving in rhythm with the world. We stop fighting the very forces that sustain us. We align.

REFLECTION: A PRACTICE OF ALIGNMENT

Choose one small rhythm in your daily life and follow it gently.

It might be the light as it moves across your home in a single day, the soundscape at dusk, the temperature shift when you open a window, or the birds that visit your yard or balcony.

Watch it without trying to influence it. Notice what changes and what repeats.

Then ask yourself: **What would it look like for me to move with this rhythm? What is one tiny, practical, humane choice that could align me more closely with the world that sustains me?**

Let that one choice be enough for today. Sustainability begins with noticing that you are already part of the Earth's cycles.

Practice: The Sustainable Gesture

Let sustainability be a form of relationship, not discipline. Once each week, choose a single act that helps life circulate more freely through your home:

- replace one item with a natural material that breathes
- compost your kitchen scraps so the soil can continue its work
- use light during the hours when light is abundant
- repair or mend something instead of replacing it
- plant something native and watch who arrives

Let the gesture be small, almost ceremonial. Offer it the way you might feed a companion being. Gently, consistently, without self-judgment. Do it as an act of reciprocity, a quiet acknowledgment of the systems that sustain you. One gesture is enough. Rhythms grow from repetition.

PRACTICE: THE REPAIR RITUAL

Once a month, tend to something that has frayed, loosened, or weathered with time.

It might be a seam that needs mending, a fence board softening at the edges, a garden bed that needs reinforcing, a birdhouse leaning slightly off-center, or a loose hinge, a cracked pot, a shared community space.

Let the act be modest but embodied. Remember that repair is not correction. It is a restoration of flow. It returns movement to what has stalled, breath to what has been neglected. As you mend, notice how your own body responds and how the simple act of restoring coherence outside often restores something subtle inside.

Repair is a practice of belonging. A way of saying: *I am part of this place, and this place is part of me.*

There is one more layer to alignment that we rarely name, perhaps because it is harder to look at directly. That layer is the material metabolism of a home. Every dwelling, no matter how small, is a point of exchange between the human world and the living Earth. Things enter our homes from somewhere. Things leave our homes to go somewhere. And these unseen streams of products, chemicals, plastics, food, water, and heat shape the health of our bodies and the health of the world with equal intimacy.

To understand a home as part of an ecosystem, we must understand it as the metabolism of materials and an alchemy of arrivals, accumulations, and returns. To understand that is to see a new kind of Feng Shui that reaches beyond the arrangement of rooms to the living heartbeat of matter itself. What arrives. What lingers. What departs.

CHAPTER TWENTY-FOUR

THE METABOLISM OF A HOME

One night, I took the trash out later than usual. The moon was a thin slice, the street quiet. I wheeled the bin to the curb and lifted the lid. The garbage was full of small, anonymous shapes. Crinkled wrappers. Plastic clamshells. The hollow bones of consumer packaging. In the dim light, the contents looked almost organic, like some strange pale fruit, tightly wrapped and waiting to be carried off.

We talk about the home as a sanctuary, as a place of protection and care. Feng Shui invites us to consider the flow of energy through rooms, the way light and air move, the placement of objects and doors. But every home is more than just the air and feeling inside its walls. Every home is part of a larger metabolism. Things coming in from somewhere. Things going out to somewhere else.

Nothing in a house appears from nowhere. Nothing in a house disappears into nowhere. Every object has a lineage. Every bin has a destination.

We live inside these flows, often without seeing them.

If we could trace the path of a single plastic container on the kitchen counter, the sturdy, clear one that held berries for a day or two, it would take us far beyond the house. Back to a refinery where fossilized sunlight was turned into resin. Back further, to rock formations holding ancient carbon, drilled and extracted. Back further still, to prehistoric forests and plankton whose bodies became the oil we now burn.

By the time the berry container arrives in our home, its story has already crossed oceans and epochs. It has passed through conveyor belts, warehouses, and trucks. It has traveled farther than most birds migrate in a year.

We bring it in without thinking, because we are hungry and berries are good. There is nothing wrong with hunger. But the container will outlive our meal by centuries.

In modern homes, the list of arrivals is long. Some inflows bring unwelcome guests. Nonstick pans are slick with coatings that flake while cooking. Carpets and couches are treated to resist stains but not bodies. Cleaning sprays whose fragrances linger in our lungs long after the shine has faded. Lotions and shampoos. Paints and sealants. Treated fabrics. Glossy receipts. Plastic-wrapped everything. Each contains a smorgasbord of man-made chemicals.

Some of these we've come to call "forever chemicals." PFAS and their cousins are substances that resist decay and travel easily through water, air, and blood. They are remarkable, in a way. They are a form of matter that refuses to join the cycles that all other things obey. From an ecological Feng Shui perspective, they are Qi that won't move on. They accumulate instead of circulate.

This isn't a confession booth. Most of us did not choose these substances with complete understanding. They arrived as part of the invisible bargain of modern life. Convenience at the front door. Complexity at the back.

The body is relationally intelligent. It responds to what enters. Our lungs react to aerosols. Our hormones listen to molecules that mimic their signals. Our nervous systems register the cumulative strain of living in a fog of low-level toxins, even when we can't name the source.

And the field beyond the house responds, too.

What we wash down the drain doesn't vanish. It joins rivers. It enters wetlands where herons stalk and red-winged blackbirds nest. It travels out into oceans where seabirds skim the surface, mistaking floating bits of plastic for food.

Early one morning, walking beside a reservoir not far from home, I watched a gull fussing over a tangle of trash caught in a branch. It pulled and shook, tugged and dropped, then tried again. From a distance, the mass looked like dried water weeds. Up close, it was a snarl of plastic bags, fishing line, and something that might once have been the strap of a sandal. The bird was searching for edible bits in what we had discarded.

For many shorebirds and seabirds, plastics are already part of the diet they feed their young. Bright fragments catch the light like fish scales. Soft pieces mimic squid. The parent returns, mouths full, to the nest and offers this false abundance to its chick. The chick's body responds as bodies do. It receives what is offered. It grows around the indigestible, carrying our convenience in its gut.

Meanwhile, in cities, crows and starlings weave cigarette filters and candy wrappers into their nests. A nest used to be a cradle of grass and twigs, lined with feathers and moss. Now, it may also hold threads of polyester and torn plastic film. Birds are not making bad choices. They are working with what surrounds them. They are reading the world we have created and responding with the same resourcefulness they have always shown.

Our "away" is their "here."

Every home is part of that story. Every bag carried to the curb joins some other landscape. Every load of laundry releases microfibers into water systems. Every chemical poured down a drain travels into creeks and rivers where ducks dabble and swallows skim.

Again, this is not about blame. It is about our relationship to our environment.

If a house is part of an ecosystem, then its metabolism, inputs, and outputs are part of that ecosystem too. Our choices are not isolated. They are streams feeding into larger rivers of impact.

Animism reminds us that everything is alive because everything is in relationship. Even objects we consider "inert" have a kind of interiority. Not human thought, but a pattern of responsiveness, a way of entering into and altering relationships.

A plastic bottle does not think, but it participates. It changes the behavior of water when it floats in it. It fills the stomach of a bird, shifting that bird's growth. It breaks into smaller and smaller fragments that lodge in gills, roots, and lungs. A PFAS molecule does not dream, but it is not nothing. It moves through a body, settles, resists breakdown, and in doing so affects what that body can become.

From this perspective, the "things" in our homes are not passive. They are participants in the field of life.

So are the alternatives.

A wooden bowl that slowly wears down, returning eventually to soil, participates differently than a plastic one that fragments but never becomes earth. A wool blanket that can be mended and later composted participates differently than a synthetic fiber that sheds microplastics with each wash.

The question isn't just: Does this item spark joy? It's also: **How does this item move through the world? What relationships does it create or strain? How will it leave?**

One of the quiet mercies in all of this is that what is gentlest for our bodies is almost always gentler for the wider world. When we choose a pan without nonstick coatings that leach forever chemicals, we are protecting our own blood and also reducing demand for substances that persist in rivers. When we pick a cleaner that doesn't burn our lungs, we're easing our own breathing while also sending fewer toxins into the wastewater that flows toward wetlands and estuaries. When we prefer natural fibers, we reduce the microplastics that wash out to sea and lodge in the bellies of fish and the tissues of seabirds.

Our health is not separate from the Earth's health. They are different expressions of the same field.

Feng Shui, in its most profound sense, is not just about arranging furniture. It is about aligning with flows that support life. In this era, that alignment must include material flows: the invisible rivers of chemicals, plastics, and waste that move through our homes as surely as air and light.

To ask, "Does this nourish me?" is also to ask, "Does this nourish or burden the watershed, the soil, the birds?"

Perceptual reverence becomes a form of health care, for ourselves and for the world.

It is easy, faced with all of this, to feel overwhelmed or defensive. The scale of the problem is vast. No one's home is free of plastic, or forever chemicals, or waste. We are embedded in systems much larger than individual choice.

The point is not purity. Purity is another kind of performance. The point is participation.

We cannot instantly undo the metabolism of global industry. But we can begin to see our homes as part of that metabolism, and to shift what we can, where we can, with the same tenderness we bring to rearranging a room for better light. Responsibility, in this sense, is not about guilt. It is about responsiveness. It asks: **Given what I now see, how might I move differently?**

Sometimes that looks like choosing glass or metal over plastic when possible, buying less and repairing more, airing out rooms and using simpler cleaners, supporting policies and companies that reduce PFAS and plastic production, or simply bringing a refillable bottle instead of relying on single-use ones.

None of these acts makes us saints. They make us participants.

And they add up, not just in their direct effects, but in the way they retrain our perception. We begin to notice labels. We learn the names of chemicals. We notice how our body feels after using a certain product, or how a room smells when we open the window instead of spraying something.

We become, in a sense, better readers of Qi. Not just subtle energy, but material energy too. We begin to see our homes from a bird's perspective, not just from above, but in terms of flow. From this vantage point, our homes look less like boxes and more like living beings.

Water comes in, water goes out. Materials arrive. Materials depart. Heat moves through.

Scent, smoke, invisible particles slip out of vents and cracks, joining the larger weather.

A house digests both matter and meaning.

When rain falls on the roof, it gathers and moves into gutters, downspouts, and into soil or storm drains. When we wash dishes, the grease and soap travel into pipes, then into treatment plants or rivers. When we take out the trash, we are redirecting a stream into landfills, where gulls, crows, and wind will greet it.

Along coastlines, albatross and shearwaters ingest our plastic and carry it across oceans. In cities, pigeons and crows forage in our landfills. In wetlands, ducks and geese feed in waters that hold both nutrients and pollutants, their health a reflection of the chemistry we send downstream.

To practice ecological Feng Shui is to widen our awareness of these flows. To ask not only how energy feels in this room? But also**, where does this water go? Where does this bottle end up? Where did this object come from?**

When we see the house as a metabolizing being, new design questions arise. **Can some of what leaves the house return to soil safely through compost, greywater, and biodegradable materials? Can we reduce the need for and use of plastic and toxins that have no good place to rest? Can we create small eddies of restoration where the house's metabolism aligns more closely with the Earth's cycles? A rain garden? A native planting? A chemical-free corner?**

These are not all-or-nothing questions. They are directional ones. They point toward alignment, not perfection.

Birds can show us what alignment could look like.

When swallows build their nests from mud and straw, those materials return to earth at the season's end. When a warbler uses spider silk, moss, and down to form a cradle, every component can re-enter the cycles of decay and renewal. These nests are intensely crafted, deeply purposeful, and yet entirely biodegradable.

A nest is a temporary structure built in full faith that the world can receive it back.

Our homes will never be as simple as this. Our lives are woven into technologies and materials that cannot yet be easily unmade. But we can let the birds remind us to move toward dwellings that are more compostable than toxic, more cyclical than permanent in the wrong ways. We can move, step by small step, from a metabolism of accumulation to a metabolism of circulation.

In Feng Shui, blocked energy is not evil. It is stuck. The remedy is not punishment but movement. Opening. Clearing. Reorienting.

Material flows work the same way.

Some substances, once loosed into the world, have nowhere to go but into deeper and deeper accumulation in sediments, in bodies, and in the very air we breathe. Others can return to soil, water, and the atmosphere in ways that nourish rather than harm.

When we choose flows that can return, the materials that can safely decompose, and products that don't leave toxic residues, we are practicing a kind of energetic hygiene at the material level. We are making it easier for the Earth's own cycles to do what they've always done: transform, renew, recombine.

What's good for our bodies is good for birds, for wetlands, for oceans. What's breathable for us is breathable for the world. Slowly, almost imperceptibly, this shifts the felt sense inside the home as well. There is less sharpness in the air. Less synthetic heaviness. Rooms begin to smell more like wood and sunlight and soup and rain, less like solvents and artificial scent.

Our bodies notice. They soften. They trust the home a little more.

And perhaps, somewhere beyond the curb, a gull finds less plastic in the tangle at the reservoir's edge.

REFLECTION: TRACING THE FLOWS

Choose one ordinary object in your home, something small enough to hold in your hand. A mug. A bottle of shampoo. A grocery item in its packaging. A cleaning spray. A favorite shirt.

Sit with it for a moment.

Let yourself ask, gently: **Where did you come from? What was taken from the Earth for you to arrive here? What waters and hands shaped you? What journeys carried you through warehouses, trucks, stores, into my home?**

Then ask: **Where will you go when you leave my home? What stream will you join? What will your long life mean for the places and beings who will meet you next?**

Don't force answers. Let impressions arise. Let curiosity replace judgment.

When you're ready, consider one small action that aligns the next object you choose to bring home or let leave your home with flows that can return. Choose something repairable. Choose something refillable. Choose something compostable. Choose something made to circulate, not accumulate. Choose less.

Let it be simple. Let it be compassionate. This is not about purity. This is about participation.

Small adjustments in the metabolism of a home ripple outward through watersheds, landscapes, and bodies, including your own.

This is the art of material Feng Shui, restoring flow not by perfection, but by attention.

When we begin to see our homes as watersheds, as porous, living points of exchange, something else becomes clear. The metabolism of a single house doesn't end at the property line. It joins a neighborhood, a street, a city. What drifts from our vents enters others' air vents. What runs down our drains moves into shared waterways. What we discard shapes the foraging patterns of birds and the nesting materials of urban wildlife.

MICROPLASTICS AS MODERN DUST

We tend to imagine microplastics as an ocean problem. But they are also an air problem.

A 2020 study found that microplastics fall from the sky like snow, settling on mountaintops, forests, farms, and, yes, our homes. They drift on wind currents just as pollen does. They ride thermals the way gulls ride updrafts.

Where the wind slows, plastic dust gathers. Where the wind funnels, it travels.

Birds navigate by these same air currents. They read subtle differences in lift, warmth, and turbulence. They soar in the very layers where microplastics now accumulate as a new kind of particulate weather.

In that sense, microplastics are the shadow side of Qi. They are an emergent, human-made substance that now moves through the same channels as life-giving breath.

This is not a call to fear. It is a call to understanding.

We can reduce plastic dust in our homes by choosing natural fibers, washing synthetics less often, line-drying when possible, and bringing in fewer single-use plastics. These choices are good for the body because they're good for the air.

The atmosphere is shared. Breath is shared. What circulates in the home circulates in the world.

In Feng Shui, the quality of Qi shapes the quality of life. In ecology, the quality of air shapes the fate of species.

In truth, they are the same teaching.

PFAS AND THE HIDDEN CURRENTS OF WATER

PFAS, those so-called "forever chemicals," move through the world quietly and persistently the way underground streams do. They follow the pathways water takes. When a nonstick pan flakes, when waterproof coating wears off a jacket, when stain-resistant spray settles into carpet fibers, tiny molecules slip into the watershed.

They do not break down. They do not rest. They simply travel.

Some remain in soil. Some ride groundwater into rivers. Some drift through storm drains, slip into treatment plants unequipped to filter them, and move onward into lakes, marshes, and coastal estuaries.

Eventually, they reach the bodies of frogs, minnows, herons, and raptors. Researchers now find PFAS in the eggs of songbirds and eagles, in the livers of fish, and in the tissues of marine mammals. Not because these beings lived near factories, but because water delivered the molecules to them.

Birds remind us that we live downstream from ourselves.

Water does not distinguish between domestic and wild, between human and nonhuman, between "us" and "environment." It simply circulates, carrying what we release.

What goes down the drain goes into the river. What enters the river enters the marsh. What enters the marsh enters a heron. And what enters the heron eventually enters us again.

Because PFAS now move through the same circulatory system that sustains all life, they are being found in human bodies as well. In the blood of nearly every person tested, across age, region, and lifestyle. In the umbilical cord blood of newborns, long before a child takes its first breath. In breast milk, the earliest food we offer. In drinking water for millions of households. In dust inside our homes, carried by fabrics, coatings, and degraded materials

None of this is a reason for shame. It is a reason for clarity.

We are not separate from the world's waters. They become us.

PFAS act as a stark teacher of ecological Feng Shui. Whatever moves through water moves through life. Whatever moves through life becomes part of the field. Whatever becomes part of the field shapes health, behavior, perception, and fate.

And yet, the teaching does not end in despair. Every reduction in treated fabric, every avoided coating, every shift to safer cookware lightens the burden of PFAS on rivers, wetlands, birds, and ourselves. We can participate in cleaner flows. In this way, even the smallest choice becomes a gesture of care for the shared body of water we inhabit together.

CHAPTER TWENTY-FIVE

THE CITY'S LIVING FLOW

A home is a dot in a much larger domain, a tiny cell in the enormous body of a city. Cities, too, have inputs and outputs, currents of wind and heat, patterns of refuge and scarcity, corridors of life pulsing between buildings.

If a home has a metabolism, then a city is a great body made of many homes, each one breathing in and out. It is a flow we live inside of.

Electricity enters at the edges, through substations, transmission lines, and grids. It threads under streets and through walls, emerging as the glow of lamps, the hum of refrigerators, and the quiet thrum of chargers. Any given flick of a switch feels trivial. Taken together, millions of small gestures become weather. Heat islands swelling over downtown. The nightly brightening of the sky. The drawdown of distant reservoirs feeding hydropower. The burning of coal or gas in plants beyond the horizon.

Water arrives through aqueducts, wells, and reservoirs. It rushes through mains to our taps, becomes tea and soup and baths and dishwater and steam. Then it disappears down drains, carrying with it shampoo, detergent, grease, traces of medication, microplastics, and everything else that has joined its body. Beneath the streets, sewage flows like an underground river, out toward treatment plants, rivers, and oceans.

Food surges in along highways and rail lines, through distribution warehouses and grocery stores. Carrots, oranges, beans, rice, bread, meat, coffee, and chocolate. Each bite carries the memory of another locale's soil, sun, labor, and fuel. What isn't eaten becomes trash or compost, joining yet another stream flowing outward to landfills, to incinerators, and to gardens and community plots where peelings and stems are returned to earth as soil.

Materials arrive and depart in constant tides. Concrete. Lumber. Steel. Clothing. Furniture. Electronics. Packages slide through fulfillment centers and onto porches. Trucks haul away the husks of broken appliances, demolished buildings, and discarded sofas.

The city inhales resources. The city exhales waste.

In most metropolises, this current is largely linear. Take, make, discard. But life, in its longest memory, prefers circles.

In a city with linear flow, energy is drawn from distant oil wells and burned once. Materials are extracted, processed, used briefly, then buried or scattered. Wastewater is treated as something to be moved away as quickly as possible, channeled into concrete drains, and whisked away from sight.

In such cities, Qi languishes in unfortunate ways. Noise accumulates in canyons of glass and steel, trash accumulates in vacant lots and underpasses, exhaust accumulates along freeways and busy arterials, and stress accumulates in the bodies of humans and animals trying to navigate it all.

We see it in asthma rates among children near highways, heat-related illnesses in neighborhoods without trees, reduced songbird diversity in highly polluted zones, and soils compacted to the point that water cannot enter.

From a bird's perspective, certain parts of such a city are effectively deserts. Not because nothing is built there, but because nothing life-giving flows through them.

From the air, a gull passing over such a city would see the consequences in how life gathers or doesn't. Sparse trees, overheated rooftops, streams running brown after storms, landfill mounds on the horizon populated by opportunistic birds and rodents.

A city with circular flow, by contrast, tries to remember the way forests and wetlands work.

Energy is harvested from the sun and wind and used in loops of efficiency. Water is slowed and invited into the soil through greenbelts, rain gardens, and permeable surfaces. Organic waste returns to compost and then to community gardens, feeding the next season's food.

Materials are repaired, repurposed, and recycled in ways that truly reuse their substance, not simply shift it down a chain toward eventual burial.

A circular metabolism doesn't pretend there is no waste. It simply acknowledges that in a healthy system, today's "waste" is tomorrow's meal for someone else.

Birds already live this truth.

A crow who picks at the remains of a sandwich on a park bench is participating in the city's food web, turning what we discard into feathers and flight. Swifts circling above chimneys convert insects into sleek, muscular bodies, their looping arcs revealing where insect densities are highest, near ponds, streetlights, and untended lots.

When we think of cities only as built environments, it's easy to miss the opportunities a circular flow provides. When we think of them as a living environment we are in relationship with, we can envision new options. Community gardens that transform vacant lots into food-producing patches where organic waste returns to the soil. Green roofs that hold stormwater and host birds and insects. Bike lanes and reliable public transit that shift some of the city's energy flows away from exhaust-heavy traffic. Tree-planting campaigns that soften heat islands, their leaves transpiring water back into the air.

From above, a migrating goose looking down might not know the names of these initiatives, but she would feel their effects. More water held on the land. More patches of green. More insects rising at dusk. A city easier to traverse and rest within.

REFLECTION: NOTICING THE CITY'S FLOW

The next time you move through your town or city, whether on foot, by bike, or even in a car, let yourself imagine that you are walking through the bloodstream of a great being.

Choose one or two flows to pay attention to:

- **Water**

Notice where it comes from: fountains, sprinklers, storm drains, creeks in culverts, gutters after rain. Where does it gather? Where does it vanish? Can you sense where it might carry what the city has washed into it?

- **Air**

Feel the changes in temperature and scent as you move. Hot pockets near asphalt. Cooler air beneath trees. Exhaust pooling at intersections. Where does your body soften? Where does it tense?

- **Life**

Watch where birds, insects, and street trees are thriving and where they are scarce. What does their presence (or absence) suggest about flow in that place?

- **Materials**

Notice how packages and goods move: deliveries, trash pickups, recycling trucks. What enters your neighborhood? What leaves it? Where does it all go?

As you observe, let your attention be curious rather than critical. You are learning the city's circulatory system.

Then ask yourself: What is one small way I already participate in these flows? What is one small way I might participate differently, more consciously?

It might be choosing a walking route that passes through more trees, carrying your own bag or bottle, supporting a local garden or green project, noticing and picking up a piece of trash on the way to the bus, or pausing to listen to birdsong at a stoplight instead of reaching for your phone.

And as we begin to feel the city as a living flow, we become ready for the next question. If this is the body we inhabit together, **how might we make it a better nest** for ourselves and for all living beings? That is where the birds will lead us next.

CHAPTER TWENTY-SIX
THE SHARED NEST

Cities are ecological bodies, whether we acknowledge them or not.

A friend once told me that to understand a city, one must follow its water. But I think we could just as easily follow the birds. They trace the city's patterns with their own lives. They know which alleys funnel wind upward in a useful updraft. They know where insects collect in the warm eddies at dusk. They know which blocks stay overheated after dark and which hold pockets of shade even at noon. They know where garbage accumulates, and with it, food. They know where trees soften air, where gutters drip clean water, where sheltered ledges offer refuge from sudden weather.

Birds read the city's metabolism not as an abstraction but as a lived terrain.

I once watched a pair of house wrens build a nest in the metal fold of a stoplight in the center of a busy intersection. Cars roared beneath them. Heat radiated off the pavement. Yet the birds moved with the same patience and precision they would have used in a quiet hedgerow. They gathered bits of grass, a strand of plastic ribbon, and a feather. They wedged their creation deep into the sheltering lip of the signal.

This is not uncommon. Urban stoplights unintentionally mimic the niches birds once found in cliffs or eroded riverbanks. The elevated platform keeps most ground predators at bay. The metal casing shields the nest from rain and midday heat. And at night, the small wash of artificial light gathers insects in a kind of reliable halo, a soft, accidental abundance. For insectivorous parents raising young, a streetlight can be a providential source of food.

Urban life doesn't confuse birds the way it confuses us.

They don't ask whether a place is "natural." They ask whether it supports life, whether wind behaves a certain way, whether insects gather, and whether the structure offers refuge.

Heat islands, shadow corridors, the turbulence between tall buildings, pockets of still air under eaves, the warmth stored in brick after dusk; birds read these features with a fluency we've largely forgotten. They navigate our architecture the way they navigate cliffs or forest canopies.

A city is a mosaic of overlapping microclimates, each one offering or withholding refuge.

What we call "infrastructure," birds experience as weather.

From the roof ledges where pigeons roost, the city's energy use is visible as warmth: vents breathing out heat into the winter air, parking garages warmer than the streets, the tops of certain buildings radiating like mild stoves at night. Birds gather in these pockets. They feel the leaks we ignore.

Swallows skim where air insects concentrate, often near warm facades or over water where air and liquid meet. The pattern of their flight traces, in miniature, the city's atmospheric metabolism.

And what we call "waste," birds experience as available material.

Landfills inhale trash and exhale methane, the sweet smell of decomposition rising into the air where vultures circle. The gulls that patrol landfills are reading these flows as clearly as we read a grocery list. To them, our discards are a seasonal abundance.

Sparrows pick threads from torn plastic bags, starlings carry cigarette filters to a nest, crows pry open discarded food containers with deft curiosity. They respond to our outputs as part of their own inputs. The city metabolizes through them, too.

Structure is not the same as sterility. A city can still hold sky.

Consider the starlings, those restless mathematicians of the air. In the city center, they gather in communal roosts as daylight thins. Trees, building ledges, the metal underbelly of a railroad bridge. All become their temporary villages. From there, in the violet hour, they rise in murmurations, bodies folding and unfolding through the air like a single great dense, amorphous cloud constantly shifting shape.

Their flight is not chaotic. Each bird tracks the movement of about seven of its nearest neighbors, adjusting direction and speed in a fractal choreography. They loop around buildings, dive over plazas, braid themselves through the wind tunnels created by high-rises. Their group mind is not abstract. It is relational. Each bird responds, moment by moment, to the shifting presence of the others.

This is Feng Shui in motion: alignment, responsiveness, and fluid coherence in the face of obstacles and predators.

Murmurations offer communal warmth, information exchange, and a nightly act of choosing safety together. The roosting sites the starlings select, whether warm facades, sheltered beams, dense tree canopies, illustrate their sensitivity to microclimate, to the smallest temperature gradients, to where danger can and cannot easily reach. They show us how bodies can cohere without losing themselves, how a community might move as one without any voice dominating the rest.

To see a city clearly is to broaden our attention, in the same way Feng Shui widens our awareness within a home. Not mystical. Simply perceptual. Where does the air move freely? Where does it stagnate? Where does water gather, and where does it vanish too quickly? What materials dominate? Which sounds rise and fall in predictable rhythms? Which spaces invite gathering, and which repel it? Which structures offer warmth, and which radiate only glare?

When we attend to these questions, the city begins to answer back.

We notice how trees planted in a line create a soft corridor of coolness that draws people the way a river draws animals. We notice how a well-placed bench becomes a social hearth. We notice how a vacant lot rewilds itself in just a few seasons, becoming a haven for pollinators and sparrows. We notice how air tastes different across blocks, how the rhythms of footsteps thrum at certain intersections, how certain corners always carry a faint scent of baking bread, diesel, or lilacs.

We become students of flow, not just residents in a grid.

And that noticing changes how we belong. Suddenly, the city is no longer an abstract system, but a living presence capable of health or sickness, capable of resilience or exhaustion. A body whose well-being is tied to ours.

Feng Shui becomes civic when we understand that alignment and flow are not confined to interiors. They are properties of neighborhoods, plazas, transit lines, rivers, sewer systems, tree canopies, wind patterns, and the daily migrations of people.

When we design for connection, we design for flow. Social flow. Ecological flow. Emotional flow. Community is a kind of shared Qi. It circulates most freely in places where people feel seen, welcomed, and safe.

Birds know how to build shared worlds.

Every murmuration of starlings shows us how bodies can attune to each other, how a collective can weave through obstacles with grace. Wrens show us how to create a home within the folds of a bustling landscape. Kestrels teach us how to see from above and how to perch in stillness long enough for the city's subtle movements to reveal themselves.

Perhaps cities could learn from the birds. Perhaps we could, too.

To move through an urban world with sensitivity is to return perception to its ecological roots and participate in its aliveness. Becoming conscious of the flows we contribute to, the flows we benefit from, and the flows we might gently redirect.

And this awareness prepares us for a deeper truth. Cities are continually co-created by birds, winds, waters, insects, soil microbes, migrating seeds, weather patterns, and the countless small decisions of countless beings. In that sense, the city is already a shared nest.

And once we feel its living flow, once we sense the currents that bind home to neighborhood, neighborhood to watershed, watershed to migrating wings, then the next step is natural. We ask how we might inhabit this shared nest with greater reciprocity, greater curiosity, and greater attention.

REFLECTION: READING THE CITY AS HABITAT

The next time you walk through your neighborhood, or even simply step outside your door, let yourself imagine the city the way birds do. Not as structures and streets, but as a living field of currents, sounds, and shelter. Choose one small practice of noticing:

- **Follow the wind as it moves around buildings.**

Feel how it funnels through alleys, softens behind corners, and gathers warmth near stone walls. Where does it flow freely? Where does it stall?

- **Watch the places where birds pause.**

A streetlight, a fire escape, a ledge warmed by the afternoon sun. Ask what makes that perch a refuge.

- **Listen for the layers of sound.**

The mechanical hum beneath the brighter thread of birdsong. What rhythms coexist in the same space?

- **Pay attention to movement.**

A wren slipping into the crevice of a stoplight. A starling flock turning as if sharing a single breath. A kestrel scanning from a traffic pole. What possibilities do they reveal about the city's hidden pathways?

As you notice, let yourself soften into the understanding that **cities, too, are ecosystems,** alive in their own relational ways. Even here, flow is possible. Even here, alignment is possible.

Then ask yourself: What is one small way I might move through my city as a participant rather than a passerby? A gesture of attention? A habit of walking instead of rushing?

A corner you look at anew?

Let that one act become your way of entering the shared nest, the place where human and more-than-human lives weave the city into a living whole.

CHAPTER TWENTY-SEVEN

CONNECTIVITY IN A FRAGMENTED WORLD

When the land is whole, Qi is good, life thrives. Water drifts from the high country to the marsh. Seeds travel on wind, fur, and feathers. Deer trails cross prairies into woodland shade. And birds, those tireless navigators of the hemispheres, follow ancestral paths across continents, pausing where food is abundant and shelter kind.

For birds, the world is not mapped by jurisdictions but by passages. A sky-road from the Arctic tundra to the Yucatán, a wind corridor from prairie wetland to high desert plateau, or a seam of coastline stitched with estuaries that provide rest in predictable intervals.

Across much of the world now, the land is no longer whole. Its continuity has been cut apart. A bird sees a mosaic of interruption along its flyway: agriculture, subdivisions, highways, malls, industrial corridors, fenced properties, golf courses, mines, airports, and scattered preserves isolated like islands in an asphalt sea.

A forest becomes a cluster of wooded scraps between subdivisions. A grassland becomes a narrow median between highways. A wetland shrinks to a retention pond tucked behind a shopping center. From above, what once was a living tapestry has unraveled into threads too thin to hold.

Ecologists call this habitat fragmentation, the breaking of once-connected ecosystems into isolated patches. From a Feng Shui perspective, broken landscapes are said to harbor *Po Qi,* wounded energy. Places where the Qi cannot gather, cannot flow, cannot nourish.

Fragmented habitats carry that same woundedness. Yin and Yang lose their dialogue. The five elements of wood, fire, earth, metal, and water no longer support one another in their ancient cycle of transformation. The land ceases to function as a coherent whole, and life weakens in the gaps.

Ecologists estimate that these fragmented landscapes lose between 13 and 75 percent of their species, not because life stops trying, but because living beings cannot cross the distances between what remains. And what remains is small. Only 5% of the lower 48 United States are pristine and intact.

Birds feel this rupture in their bones. Migration is not optional. It is a deep, inherited mandate.

Imagine, for a moment, that you were the migrant required to cross the continent. Not for recreation, not for adventure, but for survival. Once, there were plentiful full-service rest stops and hotels along the route. Places to refuel, to drink, to rest, and recover your strength. But little remains. What's left are scattered fragments. A vending machine here, a lonely gas station there, a patch of shade behind an abandoned building. You would arrive at your destination depleted, ragged, and starved for what should have sustained you along the way.

This is the world many migratory birds now navigate. Flyways, the great aerial highways stretching from the Arctic tundra to the tropics, once shimmered with wetlands, prairie potholes, rich river corridors, and forests full of berries and insects. Now those routes are broken by highways and subdivisions, wind turbines and skyscrapers, industrial fields stretching mile after mile. Birds collide with glass, lose access to open water due to drought, and arrive at stopover sites only to find them paved, polluted, or drained.

The smallest winged travelers suffer most. Bees, butterflies, moths, the soft-bellied pollinators whose flight is measured not in continents but in backyards, cannot cross the asphalt deserts between isolated gardens. Their journeys, once gentle circulations through fields of native plants, now end far short of their intended destinations. A monarch searching for milkweed encounters row after row of herbicide-treated crops.

Fragmentation is not simply the loss of habitat. It is the loss of *connection* between habitats and the pathways through which life moves, breeds, learns, and remembers itself. For animals who must travel on foot, fragmentation is brutal. Roadkill on highways is not just an individual tragedy. It is the visible edge of a larger breaking.

Fragmentation is a condition that invites response. Isolation, whether ecological or personal, is not the natural state of things. Life longs for connection. The health of any place depends on what it is connected to.

There is not enough protected land on Earth to sustain the full tapestry of life. National parks, wildlife refuges, pristine forests are often isolated islands in a vast sea of development. It's unlikely that more will be created. **If nature is to continue, it must do so with us, not in spite of us.**

Early practitioners of Feng Shui understood this intimately. Their world was not "them or us" but "us and them," humans nested within the larger pattern of the living landscape.

If the land is fragmented, then the work is connection. And connection can begin on the smallest scale.

A single native plant on a balcony becomes a flowering oasis for a fatigued bee. It's the human equivalent of a vending machine offering cold water at the edge of a desert. A container garden on a rooftop becomes a miniature rest stop for migrating songbirds. A backyard planted with keystone species becomes a bed-and-breakfast for caterpillars, warblers, and finches, all the travelers whose bodies depend on specific plants to nourish them.

Think again of the traveler on that desolate cross-country trip. If the Grand Hotel is full, the Bitsy B & B just down the street becomes salvation. If the five-star restaurant has run out of food, the Tiny Taco Stand will do just fine. Small offerings become precious in a landscape of scarcity.

The remedy for fragmentation is within our reach. Connection can be rebuilt. Our landscapes can remember wholeness. The scale of the damage is vast. But so is the scale of possibility.

A hedgerow restored becomes a passageway. A backyard planted with native species becomes a waypoint. A rooftop garden. A pocket park. A schoolyard prairie. A corporate rain garden. Each provides vital sustenance.

Wildlife travelers only need a lifeline of rest stops, tiny sanctuaries, pieces of the original pattern reassembled across backyards, balconies, and city blocks. One square foot of goldenrod or milkweed or native sage can mean the difference between survival and collapse for pollinators passing through. One shrub bearing fruit can be the meal that pushes a migrating bird to the next stopover site. One patch of unmanicured leaf litter can shelter overwintering moth pupae. Small is not symbolic. Small is real.

Every person has different resources of time, money, space, and degree of control over where they live. Not everyone has acreage. Many do not even have yards. But nearly everyone can offer something. A pot of native aster on a balcony. A window box of coneflower. A parking-strip garden replacing turf with keystone species. A little corner allowed to go wild. These gestures knit the land back together.

They create corridors. Not grand wildlife highways, but threads of life that reconnect the torn fabric. Birds and pollinators do not require perfection. They require possibility. A chain of small nodes, each only a few feet wide, can become a functional pathway across a city or suburb. Life knows how to follow such threads.

Habitat connectivity is Feng Shui at the landscape scale. It restores flow. Not metaphorical flow, but the literal movement of bodies, genes, water, pollen, and breath across space. It invites Qi to circulate again through broken places. It reopens channels for life.

Every time we offer a little more nectar, a little more shade, a little more refuge, we are mending the land's interrupted conversation. We are participating in the world's attempt to breathe again.

And perhaps that is the deepest teaching. Connectivity is not just an ecological principle.

It is an ethic of relationship.

What we restore in the land, we restore in ourselves.

REFLECTION AND PRACTICE: A MAP OF THE POSSIBLE

Sit with the map of your region. Either the actual map or the one your memory carries. Ask yourself gently: Where could one small green gesture reopen a pathway?

Imagine your home, your balcony, your yard, or your window box as a lantern on the migratory map, a tiny beacon along a darkened route for a butterfly or bird. Then choose one act of service that creates connection rather than isolation. Plant a native. Leave a patch of flowers that have gone to seed. Provide a bowl of water. Plant a seed. Provide a birdhouse or other refuge.

Small is not small to the one who needs it.

A bitsy B&B can save a life, feathered or otherwise.

CHAPTER TWENTY-EIGHT

ECOLOGICAL FENG SHUI - DESIGNING WITH CLIMATE, HUMILITY, AND KINSHIP

In the past, when I placed a chair to improve the flow or opened a window to refresh a room, I did not consider that every object in a home carries a story far older than my decision to bring it inside. The wood was once a forest. The clay was once a hillside. The fiber grew in a field as migrating geese passed overhead. The metal was carved from deep time. Even plastic, with all its difficulty, is ancient petroleum compressed from vanished seas.

A home is not just a shelter. It is an intersection of geologies, ecologies, histories, and hands. It is a small portion of Earth, rearranged.

To practice Feng Shui in the climate era is to remember this. What we invite into the home becomes part of the biome of our lives, **drawn from the land, and still shaping the land beyond us**. There is no separation between indoor and outdoor ecology. They are only different manifestations of a single, continuous ecological system.

Every object we bring inside has already lived a life in an ecosystem. It has been grown or mined, harvested or synthesized, shaped by weather, labor, heat, pressure, and time. It has drawn upon soil and water, air and energy, long before it crossed our threshold. When it enters the home, its story does not end. It changes context.

The materials we live with continue to act. They release or absorb chemicals, hold or shed heat, influence humidity, gather dust, and eventually move on again into wastewater, landfills, recycling streams, soil, or air. In this way, the interior of a home is not a sealed container but a small habitat nested within larger ones, participating continuously in the exchanges of the wider world.

The old masters taught that homes should be built "in harmony with the dragon," meaning in harmony with the shape and movement of the land: the slope of hills, the pull of water, the curve of wind. In our time, we must learn to build with the climate itself, with heat rising and storms shifting, with drought tightening its grip, with birds revising routes they once knew by heart.

But ecological Feng Shui is not a doctrine of austerity. It is a discipline of listening.

The first gesture in ecological Feng Shui is not placement. It is perception.

Where does light enter, and where does it hesitate? Which wall holds warmth in winter? Which corner feels lifeless because the air cannot move? Where does rain gather on the land outside your door? Which trees invite the small bodies of birds to rest?

These are not aesthetic questions. These are ecological ones.

In a warming world, the home must learn to breathe with its surroundings again. Birds model this constantly. Wrens select crevices that cradle morning warmth. Kestrels perch where they can sight prey. Swallows build where the airflow stays clean. They are reading microclimate, the same microclimate our homes participate in, whether we acknowledge it or not.

Feng Shui, when practiced ecologically, becomes less about arranging for luck and more about arranging for life. It's aligning the house with the energies that actually sustain it, such as sunlight, clean air, moderated temperatures, and materials that support rather than burden the wider world.

Every material affects the home's energy field, not only energetically but biologically.

Wood breathes with humidity. Clay cools. Stone holds heat and releases it slowly. Wool filters air. Natural fibers absorb scents rather than emitting them. Plants transpire, shaping humidity and air quality.

They are ecological functions.

By contrast, many conventional materials disrupt the home's ecology. Plastics that off-gas volatile compounds. Flame retardants and stain repellents that move into household dust. PFAS that enter bodies through air and skin. Synthetic foams that trap heat and moisture. Petroleum coatings that block walls and floors from breathing.

When we choose what enters the home, we are choosing what enters our bodies and the watershed downstream. When we choose clean air, breathable fibers, low-toxin surfaces, and natural light, we benefit our bodies and the environment.

Health is not separate from ecology. Health is an ecological state. Ecological Feng Shui asks us to consider materials not as inert objects but as participants.

Will this material break down safely when it leaves my home? Does its life cycle contribute to or relieve the burden on land, water, and air? Is it in alignment with the living systems around me, or does it oppose them?

These questions are forms of attention. Attention is a form of care. And care, offered consistently, becomes alignment.

The Five Elements Reimagined

Traditional Feng Shui speaks of Wood, Fire, Earth, Metal, and Water not as substances but as energies. As processes. As cycles of transformation. Ecological Feng Shui asks us to understand them this way again.

WOOD: Growth and Breath

In the home, Wood is not just plants or furniture. It is the presence of oxygenated air, the possibility of renewal. Native landscaping, shade trees, and ventilation all belong to this element. Birds teach this. They choose nest sites with breathable materials: with pathways of air they can trust.

FIRE: Warmth and Metabolism

Sunlight streaming through south-facing windows. A stove that heats efficiently. The electric hum of orientation in a home that uses its warmth wisely. Fire becomes ecological when it is sourced cleanly, when energy use honors the world's cycles.

EARTH: Stability and Nourishment

Clay walls, adobe, stone, wool rugs, earthen pigments. In ecological Feng Shui, Earth is anything that grounds the home in the cycles of soil and offers coolness in summer and steadiness year-round. Birds press nests into the Earth element when they choose mud for strength and insulation.

METAL: Clarity and Structure

Not only literal metal but the clarity of boundaries, the refinement of clean air, the precision of systems that work. Metal is present in the way a kestrel navigates the open air. Clean lines. Open sightlines. Structure in motion.

WATER: Flow and Adaptability

Humidity, plumbing, the way rain moves across the roofline, the way emotions circulate through a room. Water is the home's circulatory system, and on the land, it is the watershed's memory. To design with Water is to honor flow.

When we arrange a home with these processes in mind, we are not manipulating energy. We are participating in ecology.

Ecological Feng Shui must hold the realities of our time. Hotter summers. More intense storms. Smoke drifting thousands of miles. Species relocating or vanishing. Polluted indoor air. Stress accumulating in human bodies like sediment.

The home can no longer be thought of only as a refuge from the outside world. It must be a partner in resilience, for us and for the land.

We are called to make design choices that matter. Light-colored roofing that reflects heat rather than absorbs it. Shading trees positioned for summer relief. Cross-ventilation instead of sealed air. Natural fibers that moderate humidity. Rain gardens that capture runoff. Windows that track seasonal light. Materials that age gracefully rather than off-gas.

Each choice is small, but together they alter the home's energy field and the energy field beyond the home.

Feng Shui is often marketed as a way to manifest more abundance, productivity, and efficiency. But the deeper teaching suggests reciprocity.

Ecological Feng Shui is not about manipulating the environment. It is about conversing with it. It's about walking a piece of land before building on it. About listening to the rhythms of light before choosing where to work or rest. About honoring the beings who already inhabit a place. About asking what the land can hold, not what we want it to hold.

Humility becomes a design principle.

A house arranged with humility breathes with the weather instead of resisting it. It matures with the seasons. It shelters without severing. It aligns itself with the movements of place: the way wind curls around a hill, the way water gathers in a slight depression, the way a chickadee chooses a branch because the morning sun reaches it just after dawn.

Birds teach us what ecological Feng Shui looks like in practice. **Wrens** show how to build with what is offered, the found materials, sheltered edges, and crevices that already harmonize with the structure. **Swifts** teach us to follow airflow. They live entirely in the slipstreams between buildings, showing which spaces truly breathe. **Owls** teach us about quiet zones, the sanctity of stillness in a noisy world. **Kestrels** teach us about sightlines and clarity, and how an open view changes awareness. **Sparrows** teach us about community design and the wide adoption of simple, shared spaces.

When we design like birds, we design with relation. When we design with relation, the home becomes an ecological participant.

Our great task now is to choose materials, coatings, fibers, surfaces, sealants, and cleansers that participate in the flow of

Earth rather than poisoning it. This does not mean purity. It means discernment.

It means remembering that every object was extracted from somewhere and will return somewhere, and we live within the consequences of both.

Ecological Feng Shui invites us to reduce what harms and increase what supports and to use materials that decompose rather than accumulate. These are gestures of alignment, not moral superiority. They lighten the load on the house, on bodies, on rivers, on birds.

Every toxin avoided is a blessing to the watershed downstream. Every biodegradable object is a kindness to the soil.

When a home aligns with its climate, its materials, its watershed, and the beings who share its place, something shifts in the lives lived within it. People breathe differently. Birds linger longer. Light feels more generous. Air moves with ease. Stress decreases. Attention softens.

This is Feng Shui becoming reciprocity. Not arranging a home to attract luck, but arranging it to **give luck** back to the living world. Not designing homes just to protect ourselves from nature, but designing them to rejoin nature's conversation.

Ecological Feng Shui becomes an offering, a way of saying to the Earth, *I remember we are in a relationship. I remember I am shaped by your breath. May this home be a place where your rhythms are honored, not denied.*

REFLECTION: A PRACTICE OF MATERIAL KINSHIP

Choose one object in your home. Choose anything small, ordinary, or easily overlooked. A bowl. A garment. A wooden spoon. A lamp. A basket. A stone on the windowsill.

Hold it gently or place your hand near it.

Then ask: **Where did you come from? What land shaped you? What beings carried you into my life?**

Let the answers come slowly. Not as facts, but as felt sense.

Imagine the forest, field, or mountain where its materials once lived. Imagine the hands, human or more-than-human, that shaped it. Imagine the route it traveled to reach this room. Imagine where it will go after it leaves your care.

Then ask one more question: **How might I choose differently next time, so that my home participates in the healing of the world that shaped this object?**

Let the question open gently, without guilt, without urgency. Let it become a way of noticing, a soft doorway into ecological discernment.

Even one shift— choosing natural fibers, repairing what can be mended, declining what harms the watershed — is not small.

Every material becomes part of the home's breath. Every choice becomes part of the land's breath.

Let this reflection be an invitation to align both.

THE CLIMATE LISTENING PRACTICE

Birds are early messengers. Long before forecasts and weather reports, the world spoke through wings. This practice asks you to listen with them, and with your own body.

Set aside five quiet minutes. Step outside or open a window. Let yourself arrive in the atmosphere of the moment.

First, sense the air on your skin. Is it holding warmth that belongs to a different season?

Is it cooler than it should be, thin and early? Is the humidity familiar, or strange for this time of year? Your body knows more than you think. It has lived through many seasons and remembers the signatures.

As you settle, let the birds come forward. Listen not for species, but for patterns. Do the voices feel sparse, hesitant, scattered across a sky that once rang fuller? Do they begin earlier or later than you expect for this point in the year? Are they bright with clarity, or restless with an edge you can't quite name?

Listen for mood, texture, rhythm, the emotional weather carried in feathers and breath. Let the birds' chorus merge with your own sensations of the day. Notice how the air moves across your face, how the light feels for this season, how your body instinctively reads shift or stability, familiarity or displacement.

Climate speaks through wings, but it also speaks through us. Through the way a warm wind in winter unsettles something deep inside, through the way the first cold snap feels delayed, through the way your chest tightens or softens as the soundscape changes.

As you listen, you may notice not only presence but absence, the missing phrases, the quiet pockets, the silences where certain voices once lived. Let these gaps be part of the message.

Stay long enough for a subtle recognition to emerge, a sense that you and the birds are listening to the same world, the same air, the same shifting patterns.

When you feel complete, offer a quiet acknowledgment: **"I hear you. Thank you for telling the truth."**

No drama. No despair. Just attention — a form of care, a form of kinship.

Let what you heard and felt ripple gently into your next choices, as naturally as a bird adjusting its flight to changes in the wind.

When we begin to sense our homes as ecological beings, breathing with the sun and the storm, shaped by materials with long ancestral lives, something subtle awakens. The walls feel less inert. Light feels more communicative. Even dust motes drift with intention.

We start to sense what birds and old traditions have been whispering all along: **the world is not background. It is company.** It responds. It notices. It remembers.

Ecological Feng Shui is not merely a design strategy. It is an apprenticeship to a living Earth. And that apprenticeship widens naturally. Once you begin treating the home as kin, you begin seeing everything as kin.

This leads us back to the more profound truth beneath every practice, every placement, every noticing: What if we lived as if the whole world were alive?

Because it is.

CHAPTER TWENTY-NINE

LIVING AS IF THE WORLD WERE ALIVE

I did not set out to become an animist. I only set out to pay attention.

But attention, sustained over time, begins to reveal things our culture insists are impossible. A house that feels weary until the windows are opened. A tree that seems to lean closer after you greet it. A starling murmuration that turns as one body because, inside each bird, an awareness responds to the awareness of neighbors.

Life is not confined to organisms. Life is located in relationship. Consciousness moves along the filaments of connection. This is the quiet truth at the heart of Feng Shui, of ecology, of every Indigenous cosmology that's been dismissed as metaphor. **The world is animate because the world is relational.**

Wind interacts with leaves. Light interacts with walls. Birdsong interacts with our nervous system. Water interacts with stone, memory, and root.

Nothing here is inert. Everything responds.

When people ask whether I "believe" in a living world, I struggle to answer. Belief implies a stance taken ahead of experience. But animacy is not something I adopted. It is something I encountered through the door of attention. The more I listened, the more the world spoke. The more I softened, the more the land revealed its moods.

The more I noticed birds reading the microclimates of a city, the more I realized my own body was reading microclimates too. I had just forgotten the language. Living as if the world were alive is simply living as if the relationship is real. Because it is.

Homes respond when we treat them as participants rather than as containers. When I sweep a floor with reverence, the room feels lighter. Not because I imagine energy moving, but because I feel my relationship with the space shift. When I open windows at dawn to trade air with the world, my lungs and the walls both seem to exhale. When I place a chair where morning sun strikes, I sit differently, not dominating the light, but entering a conversation with it.

The house notices how we live in it. Not in the human sense of cognition, but in the way a field notices wind or water notices shape. We shape the home. The home shapes us. Both continue shaping the land.

Once, while standing at the edge of a wetland, I watched a red-winged blackbird claim the tallest cattail as if greeting me. The wind moved through the reeds in a slow chord, and for a breathless moment, the whole marsh seemed to turn toward me. Not welcoming or resisting, but registering. As if the land were saying: *You are here. I feel you.*

This is not fanciful. This is ecological. Every landscape has its sensitivities, its receptivity, its ways of responding.

When we plant native species, insects return. When we reduce toxins, amphibians reappear. When we remove obstacles to water, flow resumes. When we quiet ourselves, the land reveals its intelligence.

Birds make animacy impossible to ignore. A starling murmuration is a living demonstration that awareness is shared. A wren's scolding call is a reminder that territory is negotiated. A kestrel on a wire is the embodiment of presence, a consciousness so finely attuned to movement that even the smallest shift in air becomes information.

Birds read the world through constant conversation: with air pressure, with magnetic fields, with each other's gestures, with the pulse of seasons. They remind us what humans used to know. Perception is participation. To notice is to join.

When Feng Shui is practiced as if the world were alive, it becomes a discipline of mutuality.

You move a table not to manipulate fortune, but to harmonize with the room's breath. You plant a tree not for curb appeal, but to create a refuge for birds and shade for future summers. You reduce toxins not for perfection, but to lessen the burden on the watershed that holds the memory of your home.

Each choice becomes an act of reciprocity. Small. Humble. But real.

Living as if the world were alive does not require grand gestures. It looks like greeting the house when you enter, thanking light for its warmth, noticing which corners feel stagnant and letting air move, treating materials as kin with long histories, speaking softly outdoors at dawn, leaving seeds for winter birds, choosing objects that return to soil rather than poison it. listening for the mood of a place before you alter it, asking permission before pruning a tree, pausing before stepping onto a trail, and, importantly, acknowledging grief in the land when a habitat is lost.

These are not eccentricities. They are courtesies.

They remind us that we are never alone here. We are always in the presence of countless beings, each with its own interiority and expression.

This animism is not naïve. It does not deny loss, extinction, climate grief, or the unraveling of systems that sustain us. It neither romanticizes nature nor overlooks violence. It simply recognizes that life is deeper and wider than human categories allow. That everything participates in the world's unfolding. That consciousness is a spectrum of responsiveness, not a hierarchy of worth. That the Earth is not a resource but a relative.

To live as if the world were alive is to live with humility. With perceptual honesty. With kinship that extends beyond species. With gratitude that becomes practice. With practice, that becomes care. With care that becomes alignment.

A WAY TO WALK FORWARD

As the climate shifts around us, this way of living becomes more than philosophy.

It becomes survival.

Resilience emerges not only from technology and policy, but from relationships, from the ability to sense what the land is asking, to collaborate with other beings, to adapt with grace, to belong rather than dominate.

When we walk through the world as if it were alive, we walk in partnership. We walk remembering that our well-being depends on the well-being of forests, waters, insects, birds, and soils. We walk, remembering that our homes are small ecosystems nested within larger ones. That our breath is a continuation of Earth's breath. That our choices ripple outward into the fields of countless beings.

To live this way is not a return to the past. It is a way forward, a way of meeting the future with clarity, companionship, and a heart tuned to reciprocity.

CHAPTER THIRTY

THE CIRCLE BREATHES AGAIN

At the end of every long season, winter or grief or simple busyness, there comes a moment when something shifts. It may be small. The first call of a returning migratory bird, the scent of thawing soil, the way light lengthens by a single minute at dusk. But the shift is unmistakable. The circle breathes again. The ancient cycle of flow and renewal continues, where wind, water, land, and living beings move back into relationship.

One spring morning, just as the last patches of snow surrendered to the returning grass, I heard a meadowlark singing from the far fence line. That bright, liquid song rose into the air like a prayer made of sunlight. The world, despite everything, was still capable of music.

Wind moves. Water returns. Birds reorient themselves across continents. And we, too, can find our way back.

Feng Shui is not the art of interiors. It is the art of belonging. To home. To land. To one another. To the breathing, animate Earth.

And the Earth is still speaking. Still responding. Still inviting us back into the conversation that has always been under our feet, above our heads, and inside our very breath.

The circle breathes again. And we breathe with it.

A FINAL GESTURE

This book is not an instruction manual. It is a remembering. A remembering that the world is alive. You are alive within it. Your home is a breathing participant. Your body is a threshold. Your attention is a form of reciprocity. Your presence matters to the land. And the land, in its patience, has been waiting.

Practice: Taking Heartfelt, Informed Action

No single person can mend a planet's wounds. But each of us can widen the circle of care. We can lend our hands, our voices, our choices, to those already tending the living world with devotion.

As you reach the end of this book, I offer a few places where your agency can find a home. These are not the only ones, nor the "right" ones. They are simply organizations I have found meaningful in my own life, each working in a way that honors reciprocity, kinship, and the possibility of renewal.

Let your exploration be guided not by pressure, but by curiosity and affection. Choose what resonates. Follow what opens your chest a little. Let your care be informed, grounded, and alive.

Homegrown National Park

A community movement inviting people to restore biodiversity right where they live—yard by yard, balcony by balcony, window box by window box. It teaches that ecological healing begins at home, and that every patch of living green, planted with native species, becomes habitat, refuge, and corridor for birds, insects, and the beings who depend on them.

(*homegrownnationalpark.org*)

Plant Baby Plant

Plant Baby Plant is a new grassroots movement led by Robin Wall Kimmerer that invites people to reimagine our shared future through acts of care for the living world.

(*plantbabyplant.com*)

Planetary Health Alliance

A global coalition of scientists, physicians, scholars, and advocates working to protect both human health and the health of Earth's systems. Their work recognizes what this book affirms: that the well-being of our bodies and the well-being of the biosphere are inseparable, braided into one continuous metabolism of life.

(*planetaryhealthalliance.org*)

Garden for Wildlife

An organization that helps people create nourishing, wildlife-friendly habitats in everyday spaces. Through native plants, guidance, and ecological design, they offer simple ways to support birds, pollinators, and the web of life with beauty and practicality.

(*gardenforwildlife.com*)

The Pachamama Alliance

A collaboration between Indigenous wisdom keepers of the Amazon and allies around the world, dedicated to protecting forests, cultures, and the future of life on Earth.

Their programs invite participants into deep relational activism—action grounded in reverence, responsibility, and the understanding that we are part of a much larger living community.

(*pachamama.org*)

Let these offerings be a beginning, not a burden. A single step, taken with sincerity, joins a much larger movement toward restoration. The planet does not need you to be perfect.

It only needs you to participate—with clarity, humility, and heart.

A Closing Blessing

May you walk through the world with a listening heart.

May you feel the quiet intelligence of wind, water, soil, and stone speaking to you in their ancient dialects.

May the birds remind you that orientation is always possible, even in uncertain times.

May your home become a sanctuary not by perfection, but by relationship—a place that breathes with the land that holds it.

May you trust the small gestures. They are threads in a vast web of reciprocity.

And when the world feels heavy or fractured, may you take heart in this truth:

You are not working alone. You are working alongside forests and rivers, alongside people you may never meet, alongside ancestors who tended the land before you, alongside children and birds and seeds who are praying for a future they cannot yet see.

May your life be one small, luminous gesture of care.

May your choices be blessings to the watershed downstream.

May your presence bring ease to the spaces you inhabit.

And may the Earth, in all her patience, resilience, and remembering, feel your devotion and whisper back:

You belong. You always have.

ACKNOWLEDGMENTS

This book, like all living things, was shaped by many unseen currents, some thousands of years old. I am deeply grateful to those whose guidance and generosity have helped me find my way along the flow.

To my husband, whose faith in me has been a steady wind at my back. Thank you for believing in the worth of this work and for encouraging me to keep listening, keep writing, even when the words came slowly, frustration mounted, and tears came fast. Your presence has been its own kind of alignment.

To my family and friends near and far, named and unnamed, whose love, patience, laughter, and steady presence have held me through seasons of growth and uncertainty. This book is, at its heart, about relationships: to one another, to our surroundings, and to the living world that holds us all. Without these bonds of care and belonging, not only this book, but life itself, would lose its meaning.

To my college advisor, the late Dale Hein, who taught me that balance and humor are as essential to a good life as knowledge.

To Al LeCount, my first boss, who showed me how to read the land and the bears we studied, teaching me that every footprint, every broken twig, is part of a story worth learning.

To another boss, Bob Hernbrode Jr., who opened my eyes to the intelligence of birds and how to watch them with patience and reverence.

To all the incredible environmental educators I've worked with over the decades and those just getting their feet wet in the depths of this work, I'm proud to be a part of this tribe.

To my Feng Shui teacher, Terah Kathryn Collins, and the other instructors at the Western School of Feng Shui, whose insights reconfirmed my sense that home and nature are not separate worlds but one continuous pattern. And to my colleagues in the International Feng Shui Guild, who have broadened my understanding of how this ancient practice can evolve, still rooted in reverence, still alive with discovery.

To Mrs. Northcross, my junior high teacher, who first told me I had a gift for writing and gave me the courage to trust that voice.

To the many students I taught over the years, full of curiosity and probing questions. You taught me that nature study and ecological restoration are not lessons to learn but a relationship to enter. Your joy, your reverence, and your willingness to care and challenge convention have shaped me more than you know.

To Barb Horn, a former colleague who formed the Riverwatch program, that engaged communities and students in the care and protection of Colorado's precious waters. My students loved the program, which continues to this day. Barb is now a life coach extraordinaire, continuing her efforts to help others reach their full potential.

To my beta readers: Lynnette Baumann, Dianne Pavelka, Crystal Andrews, and Debbie Alther. Thank you for your careful attention, your thoughtful questions, and your generous suggestions. Your willingness to sit with these words, to test their clarity and truth, helped this book become stronger, more grounded, and more fully itself.

To the long-standing book group that includes Dianne, Crystal, and Debbie, a circle so enduring that no one remembers exactly when it began, thank you for decades of reading together, thinking together, and talking deeply about the stories that shape us. This shared devotion to books and conversation has been a quiet but constant nourishment, reminding me that writing does not happen in isolation, but in community.

To Karen Stuth and Amy Koenig from Satiama Publishing, for their guidance and belief in this work. I can only imagine the leap of faith you both must have taken to take a chance on a neophyte author with a quirky writing style and worldview. The birth of this book could never have happened without your midwifery, and certainly not have arrived in its beautiful format. Thank you for letting my heart share its deep love of Feng Shui, of nature, and of humanity.

And to Robin Wall Kimmerer, whom I have never met, yet who has been one of my most profound teachers. Her words dissolved the imagined boundaries between science, story, and spirit, allowing so many of us to speak again from the heart, from place, and from kinship with the living world.

Finally, to the birds, winds, and waters that continue to teach without words.

May we keep listening.

ABOUT THE AUTHOR

Wendy Ellen Hanophy is a wildlife biologist, writer, and educator whose work lives at the meeting place of ecology, perception, and belonging. Trained in the natural sciences, she spent years studying wildlife and teaching ecology, learning firsthand how deeply the living world is shaped not only by physical forces but also by relationships.

Her path has been shaped as much by listening as by data. By watching animals move across the land, by working with students to restore a degraded wetland behind a Colorado high school, and by co-creating an urban wildlife conservation education program that eventually connected roughly 29,000 young people yearly with the natural world, she witnessed how attention and care can heal people and places together. Guiding students as they planted native species, monitored returning birds and insects, and taught younger children, she saw how love of place is learned through the body as much as the mind.

Over time, Wendy began weaving her scientific training with a form of Feng Shui rooted in its original ecological sensibility, not as a system of rules, but as a practice of awareness. Her work invites people to see homes not as sealed containers, but as living participants in larger landscapes of wind, water, and life.

Now living on the high plains of Colorado, she continues to explore how perception shapes ecology through writing, native-plant gardening, and teaching practices that restore balance without domination. Her work is guided by a simple conviction that healing the world begins with learning to listen again.

RECOMMENDED RESOURCES FOR YOUR GROWTH AND DELIGHT

This list is not exhaustive — only a beginning.

Ecology & Place

- Robin Wall Kimmerer — *Braiding Sweetgrass*
- David Abram — *The Spell of the Sensuous*
- Barry Lopez — *Arctic Dreams*
- David George Haskell — *The Songs of Trees*
- Scott Russell Sanders — *Staying Put*
- Zoe Schlanger — *The Light Eaters*
- Douglas W. Tallamy — *Nature's Best Hope* and *How Can I Help?*

Climate Change

- Paul Hawken — *Carbon, The Book of Life* (as well as any of his books on this topic)

Feng Shui

- Terah Kathryn Collins — *The Western Guide to Feng Shui*
- Maureen K. Calamia — *Creating Luminous Spaces*

Design, Architecture, & Biophilia

- Stephen Kellert — *Birthright* and *Nature by Design*
- Christopher Alexander — *A Pattern Language*
- Janine Benyus — *Biomimicry*
- Clare Cooper Marcus — *House as a Mirror of Self*

Contemporary Animism / Relational Thought

- Tyson Yunkaporta — *Sand Talk*
- Enrique Salmón — *Iwigara*
- Sophie Strand — essays and talks on myth & ecology

Commitment and Service

- Lynne Twist — *Living a Committed Life*

SOURCES

The following bibliography is for ecologists and professional Feng Shui practitioners. This book was informed and supported by years of research into early Form School Feng Shui, drawing on academic books and papers, architectural journals, translations of ancient works, and related sources. I wanted to be sure I accurately represented the knowledge shared by those long-ago geomancers. Unlike many indigenous peoples, these early Feng Shui or Kan Yu practitioners had a written language, and some of their texts survive to the present day. It's humbling to realize how often knowledge is gained and lost, and how politics or governments can discount the vital understandings of other cultures. I relied heavily on the works of anthropologists, especially Eugene Anderson, whose book planted the seed for this one.

Anderson, E. N. (1996). Feng-shui: Ideology and ecology. In *Ecologies of the Heart: Emotion, belief, and the environment* (pp. 15–27). Oxford University Press.

- Demonstrates feng shui as an effective land-planning science and motivational force for ecological adherence.

Anderson, E. N., et al. (2018). Fengshui forests and village landscapes in China: A literature review. *Urban Forestry & Urban Greening, 31*, 79–92.

- Shows feng shui sacred groves functioning as biodiversity reserves and habitat corridors.

Beijing siheyuan. (2024, June 24). In *Wikipedia.*

https://en.wikipedia.org/wiki/Beijing_Siheyuan

- Concise overview of Beijing courtyard house layout and cultural significance.

Beijing's Si He Yuan. (2023). International Department of the CPC Central Committee.

https://www.idcpc.org.cn/english2023/chinadelights/arts/archi tecture/202307/t20230727_157781.html

- Official Chinese government explanation of siheyuan cosmology and design principles.

Brown, Tristan. (2023). Laws of the Land: Fengshui and the State in Qing Dynasty China. Princeton University Press.

- A groundbreaking history of Feng Shui's roles in public life and law during China's last imperial dynasty, with ecological and land preservation implications.

Bruun, O. (2008). A brief history of feng shui. In *An introduction to feng shui* (pp. 23–49). Cambridge University Press.

- Traces feng shui's evolution from early KanYu practices through classical schools.

Çeliker, A., Tevfikler Çavuşoğlu, B., & Öngül, Z. (2008). Comparative study of courtyard housing using Feng Shui. *Architectural Engineering and Design Management, 4*(1), 58–72.

- Compares courtyard designs using both feng shui criteria and environmental performance metrics.

Chapter three: Feng shui and contemporary environmental design. (n.d.) In *An environmental design thesis.*

https://vtechworks.lib.vt.edu/bitstream/handle/10919/29291/3_EnvPrinciples.pdf

- Maps feng shui five elements and trigrams to measurable environmental design factors.

Choe, Y., & Han, S. (2020). Applicability of Feng Shui thoughts for sustainable space planning and evaluation in Korea was verified using three-dimensional digital mapping and simulations. *Sustainability, 12*(21), 8904.

- Tests feng shui layouts using modern digital simulation for sustainability outcomes.

Chinese siheyuan architecture: A study of traditional Chinese courtyard houses. (2018, August 13). DiVA Portal.

http://www.diva-portal.org/smash/get/diva2:1238659/FULLTEXT01.pdf

- Detailed architectural analysis of the siheyuan design as a microclimatic.

Chinese traditional architecture. (2022, February 15). European Guanxi.

https://www.europeanguanxi.com/post/chinese-traditional-architecture

- Accessible overview connecting traditional Chinese homes to cosmology.

Courtyard (siheyuan). (2004, January 13). *China Daily.*

https://www.chinadaily.com.cn/english/livechina/2004-01/14/content_298861.htm

- Early English-language description of siheyuan layout and family organization.

Courtyard houses of Beijing: Lessons from the renewal field report. (2016). *Traditional Dwellings and Settlements Review, 27*(1).

- Practical lessons from modern siheyuan restoration projects.

Courtyard housing in China: Chinese quest for harmony. (2013). *International Journal of Contemporary Urban Affairs, 1*(1), 1–15.

- Explores siheyuan as embodiment of relational harmony principles.

East meets West: On Feng Shui and Western environmental

models. (2001). In *Architectural Research Centers Consortium proceedings.*

https://www.arcc-repository.org/index.php/repository/article/download/762/630

- Direct comparison of feng shui principles with Western environmental design theory.

Empirical and quantitative studies of Feng Shui: A systematic review of research trends and methodologies. (2023). *Frontiers in Psychology, 14.*

- Reviews scientific evidence supporting feng shui's environmental benefits.

Erdogan, E., and Erdogon, H. (2014). Feng shui paradigm as philosophy of sustainable design. International Journal of Social, Behavioral, Educational, Economic, Business and Industrial Engineering 8(10), 3328-3333.

- Feng Shui's importance in sustainable design and living.

Feng shui. (n.d.). In *The encyclopedia of housing* (2nd ed.). Sage.

https://sk.sagepub.com/ency/edvol/download/housing2ed/chpt/feng-shui.pdf

- Encyclopedic overview of feng shui principles and historical development.

Feng shui. (n.d.). In *Wikipedia.*

https://en.wikipedia.org/wiki/Feng_shui

- Comprehensive reference covering feng shui schools, history, and principles.

Feng Shui: A Chinese approach to integrated design. (en..). CIB / IRBnet.

https://www.irbnet.de/daten/iconda/CIB14390.pdf

- Connects traditional feng shui to modern integrated environmental design.

Feng Shui: A comprehensive review of its effectiveness based on environmental psychology and sustainable design principles. (n.d.). *International Journal of Advanced Scientific Research and Engineering.*

https://ijasre.net/index.php/ijasre/article/download/1383/1865/2643

- Synthesizes Feng Shui's alignment with environmental psychology research.

Feng Shui meets sustainability: 5 ideas for a greener future. (2023, November 28). Gensler Research & Insight.

https://www.gensler.com/blog/feng-shui-meets-sustainability-5-ideas

- Practical design firm perspective on feng shui + contemporary sustainability.

Feng Shui of hutong alleyways & siheyuan houses, Beijing, China. (2015, April 11). Malaysia Feng Shui Master.

http://malaysiafengshuimaster.com/feng-shui-of-hutong-alleyways-and-siheyuan-houses-beijing-china/

- Practitioner explanation of feng shui principles in Beijing courtyard context.

Fengshui: A moral technique-art for contemporary environmental concerns. (2023). *Asian Studies, 11*(1), 197–223.

- Frames feng shui as ethical environmental practice for modern challenges.

Global Atelier 3.0 – Feng Shui: Tracing the evolution of Chinese spatial culture. (2024, October 13). AB Design Studio.

https://www.abdesignstudioinc.com/news/global-atelier-3-feng-shui

- Architectural perspective on feng shui's evolution and spatial principles.

Guo Pu and the Book of Burial (Zang Shu). (2010, September 21). Ancient Feng Shui.

https://ancientfengshui.wordpress.com/2010/09/22/feng-shui-or-kanyu-book-of-burial-aka-zang-shu/

- Accessible discussion of foundational KanYu text and Form School origins.

Insideinside.org. (2018, January 20). Siheyuan, Beijing, China.

https://insideinside.org/project/siheyuan-beijing-china/

- Visual and architectural documentation of preserved Beijing siheyuan.

Integrating Fengshui and environmental psychology into residential landscape design. (2025). *City Diversity, 6*(1), 3036.

https://aber.apacsci.com/index.php/cd/article/viewFile/3036/3649

- Merges feng shui placement rules with environmental psychology metrics.

Jiang, P. (Ed.). (1999). *Five classics of fengshui*. Brill.

- English discussion of classical feng shui texts, including Zang Shu.

Lu, X. S., & Zhen, X. S. (2013). Fusion study on architecture Feng-Shui theory and ecological architecture of Edong ancestral hall. *Advanced Materials Research, 671–674*, 2198–2202.

- Tests feng shui principles against modern ecological architecture criteria.

Mak, M.Y., & So, A.T (Eds.((2009). Research in Scientific Feng Shui and the Built Environment. City University of Hong Kong Press.

- Present Feng Shui as a broad ecologically and architecturally connected paradigm for architects and land managers.

Parkes, G. (2000). Winds, waters, and earth energies: Fengshui and sense of place. In S. Feld & K. Basso (Eds.), *Senses of Place* (pp. 209–230). University of Washington Press.

- Environmental phenomenology framing feng shui as embodied place relationship.

Performance of traditional Chinese courtyard buildings from a sustainability perspective. (2024, July 11). *Journal of Contemporary Architecture and Urbanism, 6*(3).

- Analyzes siheyuan microclimatic performance using modern sustainability metrics.

Siheyuan. (n.d.). In *Wikipedia.*

https://en.wikipedia.org/wiki/Siheyuan

- Comprehensive reference on siheyuan history, layout, and variations.

Siheyuan, Beijing courtyard – local traditional unique house. (2022, December 31). Travel China Guide.

https://www.travelchinaguide.com/cityguides/beijing/hutong/yard.htm

- Detailed description of classic Beijing siheyuan layout and room functions.

Su, B. (2014). Traditional Feng Shui architecture as an inspiration for the development of green buildings. *eJournal of Public Affairs, 3*(2), 40–56.

https://www.ejournalofpublicaffairs.org/traditional-feng-shui-architecture-as-an-inspiration-for-the-development-of-green-buildi

- Links feng shui courtyard design directly to modern green building principles.

Tallamy, D. W. (2019). *Nature's best hope: A new approach to conservation that starts in your yard.* Timber Press.

- Shows how ordinary yards can become a biodiversity habitat, supporting homegrown conservation.

The essence of KanYu in feng shui and the emperor valley of the East. (2021). *Prajñā Vihāra, 22*(1), 110–122.

https://assumptionjournal.au.edu/index.php/PrajnaVihara/article/download/5549/3122

- Explores early KanYu practices and their environmental foundations.

The origin, history & different schools of feng shui. (2014, May). Taoist Sorcery.

http://taoist-sorcery.blogspot.com/2014/05/feng-shui-origin-history.html

- Practitioner overview of feng shui schools, including Form School origins.

Xu, P. (1998). Feng-shui models structured traditional Beijing courtyard houses. *Journal of Architectural and Planning Research, 15*(4), 271–282.

https://lockescience.com/files/Xu.pdf

- Definitive scholarly analysis of siheyuan feng shui, including Lu Ban proportions.

Xu, P. (2021). Applying systems philosophy: General models integrating architecture with landscape design to create a sustainable built environment in light of feng-shui. *Open House International.*

- Systems ecology approach to feng shui landscape design principles.

MORE FROM SATIAMA PUBLISHING

Non-Fiction Books

A Speckled Stone by Karen Stuth

Ancient Sky Watchers & Mythic Themes (A Sky Lore Anthology Volume One) by Julie Loar*As Above, So Below: Sun, Moon & Stars* (Sky Lore Anthology Volume Two) by Julie Loar

The Essence of Sound: Full Spectrum Vibrational Healing for the Meridians, Chakras, Auric Field & Figure Eight Energies by Evelyn Mulders

Symbol and Synchronicity: Learning the Soul's Language in Dreams and Waking Life by Julie Loar

The Truths of Tula by Dianna Cates Dunn

Three Awakenings: A Spiritual Memoir by Theresa Crater

Born of Stars, Awakened on Earth: A Galactic Guide for Starseeds by Arielle Taylor & Lavandar

Navigating Your Shadow: An Intuitive Compass for Exploration by Liz O'Connor

Unspoken Costs: How To Have Relationship-Saving Money Conversations by Vivian Cobb

Fiction Books

My Uncle Owes Me a Favor by Morrigan Milligan

Children's Books

Extraordinary O Finds Her Superpower by Sara Bloomfield & Amy Sachse

Magic on the Mountainside by Nancy Godbout Jurka

The Invisible Riptide by Carron Montgomery

Violet's Gone Viral by Anne Waugh Moore

Coming Soon

The Real Truth About Lena by Carron Montgomery, Karen Stuth and Amy Koenig

Extraordinary O and the Case of the Missing Pup

Sara Bloomfield & Amy Sachse

E-books

Symbol and Synchronicity: Learning the Soul's Language in Dreams and Waking Life by Julie Loar

How the Trees Got Their Voices by Susan Andra Lion

The Essence of Herbs: A Meridian Approach to Physical and Emotional Well-being Using Nature's Wisdom by Evelyn Mulders

The Essence of Sound: Full Spectrum Vibrational Healing for the Meridians, Chakras, Auric Field & Figure Eight Energies by Evelyn Mulders

Three Awakenings: A Spiritual Memoir by Theresa Crater

Children's E-books

Magic on the Mountainside by Nancy Godbout Jurka

The Invisible Riptide by Carron Montgomery

Violet's Gone Viral by Anne Waugh Moore

Extraordinary O Finds Her Superpower by Sara Bloomfield & Amy Sachse

Audio Books on CD

Children's Spirit Animal Stories Vol I by Dr. Steven D. Farmer

Children's Spirit Animal Stories Vol II by Dr. Steven D. Farmer

Card and Tarot Decks

Children's Spirit Animal Cards by Dr. Steven D. Farmer with Jesseca Camacho

Cosmic Cat Wisdom Deck by Randy Crutcher and Barbara J. Horn

Divine Dog Wisdom Deck by Randy Crutcher and Barbara J. Horn

The Wisdom of Tula by Karen Stuth, Art by Dianna Cates Dunn

Whispering Herbs Healing Card: Essential Wisdom from Mother Earth by Evelyn Mulders

Coming Soon

Shadow Animal Oracle Deck by Liz O'Connor

Games

Quintangled: A Game of Strategy, Chance & Destiny by Julie Loar, Susan Andra Lion, and Karen Stuth

Meditation and Music CDs

Come Walk With Me: Four Meditation Journeys to Becoming Your Higher Self by Eva Black Tail Swan

Safe Passage by Trina Brunk

SIGN UP TODAY

Sign up for our newsletter and hear more from our authors and us, and learn about our newest releases first!

SIGN UP FOR OUR NEWSLETTER

Made in the USA
Coppell, TX
01 August 2026

85448551R00128